THE CONFESSIONS OF
ST. AUGUSTINE
A reinterpretation of the great devotional classic

WALKING
INTO LIGHT

DAVID WINTER

Harold Shaw Publishers
Wheaton, Illinois

ISBN 0–87788–916-3

Cover illustration: Joe DeVelasco

Library of Congress Cataloging-in-Publication Data

Winter, David Brian.
    Walking into light.

    Paraphrase of: Confessions of St. Augustine.
    1. Augustine, Saint, Bishop of Hippo.   2. Christian
saints—Algeria—Hippo—Biography.   3. Hippo (Algeria)—
Biography.   4. Christian life—1960-   I. Augustine,
Saint, Bishop f Hippo. Confessiones.   II. Title.
BR1720.A9W56 1986   242   86-6619
ISBN 0-87788-916-3 (pbk.)

95 94 93 92 91 90 89 88 87 86

10 9 8 7 6 5 4 3 2 1

Contents

Introduction _____ 7

Part I

Chapter One　　Boyhood

1 Wrong Priorities and False Ambitions
  at Sixteen _____ 19
2 Why Do We Sin? _____ 20
3 A Double Mercy _____ 24
4 When Company Corrupts _____ 25

Chapter Two　　Wrestling with Truth

5 The Importance of Truth _____ 29
6 A Mother's Dream _____ 31
7 Breaking the Hold of Astrology _____ 33
8 Tears of Bitterness _____ 38
9 God of Beauty _____ 40

10 The Eternal Wisdom _____ 41
11 A Mother Prays _____ 42
12 An Important Decision _____ 45

Chapter Three   Marking Time in Milan

13 Accepting Correction_____ 50
14 My Problems with Proof_____ 52
15 No Pleasure in Sin_____ 55

Chapter Four   Friendship with Alipius

16 Obsession with Sport _____ 58
17 Another Painful Experience _____ 62
18 The Intellectual Quest _____ 64
19 When the Body Rules the Mind: The Pursuit
      of Marriage _____ 68
20 The Problem of Evil _____ 70
21 Light Begins to Dawn _____ 73
22 Misconceptions about Jesus _____ 76

Chapter Five   The Moment of Truth

23 The Last Steps: The Power of Testimony _____ 82
24 A Chain of Iron _____ 87
25 Make Me Holy . . . But Not Yet_____ 89
26 One Day in the Garden _____ 91

Chapter Six   Believing . . . and Grieving

27 The Effect on our Friends _____ 98
28 The Joy of the Spirit _____ 101
29 God's Mercy in Baptism _____ 103
30 An Occasion for Celebration_____ 104
31 The Death of My Mother _____ 107
32 Grieving and Believing _____ 110

Part II

Chapter Seven **Teacher and Preacher**

33 The Dangers of Gossip _____ 118

34 It Is Not *What* but *How* We Know
    that Matters _____ 119

35 Obeying God and Caesar_____ 120

36 The Language of the Heart _____ 122

37 What Is God Like? _____ 123

38 God and the Passing of Time _____ 125

39 Worthy to Be Praised _____ 126

40 Seeing and Believing_____ 128

41 The Pure in Heart See God _____ 130

42 The Presence of God_____ 132

43 In Search of the Land of the Happy Life ___ 135

44 A Song of Steps: A Meditation on Psalm 120 _ 137

45 Sharp Arrows of Love: A Meditation on
    Psalm 120:4 _____ 139

46 The Tents of Kedar: A Meditation on
    Psalm 120:5 _____ 141

47 The Guard Who Never Sleeps: A Meditation
    on Psalm 121 _____ 142

48 Going Out and Coming In: A Meditation
    on Psalm 121:8 _____ 144

49 The Heavenly Jerusalem: A Meditation
    on Psalm 122 _____ 146

INTRODUCTION

In the year of our Lord 354, at a town then called Tagaste (now Souk-Ahras) in the Roman province of Numidia (now Algeria), one of the outstanding figures in the history of the Christian church was born. That was Augustine of Hippo. Although not converted and baptized until he was over thirty years old, he became a priest, bishop, theologian of enormous influence, and founder of the Augustinian order.

The Roman Catholic Church has always recognized Augustine's importance, but many of the great Protestant reformers, especially Luther, also admit their debt to him as a biblical scholar and theologian. Augustine died at Hippo, where he was bishop, during the siege by the Vandals in A.D. 430.

Even given Augustine's stature as a Christian thinker, it might seem that the life and circumstances of a Latin-speaking intellectual of the fourth century has little in common with English-speaking people in our scientific and technological age. In fact, however, the points of contact are endless. Human beings in every age and culture have asked similar questions, worried about similar problems, and struggled against similar adversaries (most of them rooted in their own nature). Augustine's life story, told with remarkable frankness in his autobiographical "confessions," introduces us to a person much like ourselves.

It is true that the theological questions facing Augustine don't worry many of us today. In early manhood he became a disciple of Mani—a *Manichee*, as they were known. So for many years Augustine espoused strange beliefs about a world of primal forces of light and darkness struggling for mastery. Manichaeism had no room for a personal God and even less for the idea of a God who could take form or substance as the Christians claimed that God had done in Jesus. Augustine was concerned with the relationship between the idea of God and the nature of physical existence—not a common problem today.

Augustine was also concerned with the question

of the origin of evil, which, as he eventually came to see, the Manichees failed to answer adequately. They believed in dualism (that is, that two more or less equal forces of good and evil were competing for control of humanity and the cosmos). Augustine looked into his own heart and echoed the words of Paul, "Who will rescue me from this body of death?" He struggled to contain or overcome temptations, especially sexual ones, but he constantly failed—despising himself, and feeling powerless to do better.

Nonetheless, in Augustine's *Confessions*, we see parallels with modern problems. Augustine lived in a society that worshiped status and success. Often it regarded violence as a source of excitement or entertainment. It gave sports an exaggerated importance and the serious pursuit of spirituality very little importance at all. In Augustine's experience, the group violence of teenagers, self-indulgent sexuality, excessive respect for fashionable opinion, unwillingness to take an unpopular or minority stand on issues of principle, addiction to astrology, and insensitive attitude toward the opposite sex were at different times important influences.

As we read his book, we see the man—and he is a lot like us. Most of the moral problems he faced, we face. Most of the temptations he indulged in, and the issues on which he compromised, are still defeating or compromising us. Where human nature is concerned, there is very little new under the sun.

But most of all, Augustine's spiritual pilgrimage is like ours. He was not prepared to settle for the nominal or minimal Christianity that was widely practiced (then as now). He wanted the best, because he wanted to know God. He would not settle for anything else.

So we follow him along a tortuous and painful path. Slowly all alternatives were closed to him. He was shut in on his search, sensing that Jesus Christ was in some way the clue to it all. Still, for many years he failed to open his mind to the moral and spiritual requirements of the gospel. A brilliant thinker, for long—too long—he thought that the chief barrier to belief was intellectual. Finally, in the climax of the story, a hot afternoon in an Italian garden revealed to him that it was a matter of morality and will. *Faith* is not understanding perfectly, but trusting completely—and being ready to have done with sin.

But that is to preempt a good story. Let me at this point simply fill in enough background to enable ordinary readers to enjoy it.

The church of the fourth century was at a crossroads. After the apostolic period and the terrible persecutions that followed it, Catholic (which is simply to say "orthodox") Christianity had become established virtually across the Roman world. The Cross had had many victories, including the conversion of the Roman emperor Constantine. But those victories carried with them a price. The church, once so distinctive in its message and life-style, became part of the status quo.

It still had enemies, and bitter ones, as we shall see. The leading figures in Roman society had reverted to the old pagan religion. Various heresies plagued the church and led the uninstructed astray. For example, the Arians, who denied the physical incarnation of Jesus, and the Manichees are two heretical groups mentioned by Augustine. In many ways it was a costly and painful thing to take one's stand as an uncompromising Christian—as, I suppose, it always has been.

But the church existed, and had power, wealth, and influence. Declining for the most part to take up the Lord's command to evangelize "all the world," it was ripe for the development within its ranks of various superstitions, religious diversions, and philosophical concerns.

In particular, the church of Augustine's day had gotten itself into a strange position over baptism. Most church leaders accepted the idea that sin after baptism was essentially unforgivable (basing the idea on Hebrews 6:4-6). Consequently they preferred to delay baptism as late in life as possible, even up to a person's deathbed, in the hope that he or she would die completely free from post-baptismal sin. Augustine himself never held that view, and later in his life was a leading influence in getting the practice abandoned. He and his illegitimate son were baptized within a year of conversion, although Augustine's father Patricius, a late convert, was baptized on his deathbed.

The church at the time was being pulled two ways: toward the early church, the apostles, and the daring simplicity of their message of repentance, faith, and baptism; and toward a more hierarchical, organized, ritualistic, and legalistic kind of church, in which the primitive message was in danger of being overlaid with new, man-made traditions. Some of those struggles are reflected in the book. Augustine devoted much of his later life to promoting the pure apostolic gospel, untainted with pagan or worldly ideas.

The church of that time was also, however, experiencing spiritual renewal, especially in Egypt, and that movement, as we shall see, touched the life of young Augustine.

But the greatest influence on Augustine, greater even than that of the apostle Paul or the saintly bishop, Ambrose of Milan, whom he admired so much, was the influence of his mother Monica. If for nothing else, the *Confessions* would stand as an everlasting testimony to the character, courage, and faith of this astonishing woman. In a period of history when women were little regarded except as playthings of young men and possessions of their husbands, Monica never faltered in her belief that her husband and son would eventually share her faith. She prayed and fasted, wept and worried, but most of all she set before them an attractive example of what a Christian could be like. She was quiet, gentle, but single-minded.

Augustine's conversion came in A.D. 386, when he was professor of rhetoric at Milan—1600 years ago. A few of the churches and sanctuaries he knew still survive around the Mediterranean, mainly as ruins. The people who seemed so powerful as enemies of the faith are, for the most part, forgotten, except as names or footnotes in history books. The philosophies that tantalized Augustine, like Neo-Platonism, and the authors he admired, like Cicero, are still available for study, but are hardly regarded as credible bases on which to build an approach to life.

Yet the faith Augustine discovered for himself lives on, in its heart the same today as then: Everything offered to us by God is an unmerited favor—grace—and the means by which we receive it is always complete dependence on God—faith. *Grace through faith* opened Augustine's eyes, as it opened Luther's and Wesley's eyes, and those of many ordinary believers ever since.

Augustine nourished the grace he had received with the same sacrament that feeds us today. He eagerly read the same Bible, especially the Psalms and the letters of Paul, in his early days as a Christian. He was baptized through the same rite. He looked for and experienced the gifts of the same Holy Spirit. He longed for and saw the conversion of his closest friends.

In this paraphrased version of the *Confessions,* much of the original is necessarily omitted. My goal has been to make what in its entirety is a fairly demanding and even obscure book as accessible as possible to ordinary modern Christians. The bulk of the book is Augustine's own story, told in his own words, but freely paraphrased into modern English. Nothing is added: what you will read is, as nearly as this writer understands it, what Augustine intended to convey. The later chapters are examples of Augustine's thoughts on various spiritual, ethical, and moral topics.

I hope that this book will be rewarding, interesting, and enlightening. I hope it will be easy to read. What I am absolutely sure of is that its ideals will be anything but easy to put into practice.

PART I

CHAPTER ONE

Boyhood

Augustine grew up in a flourishing Roman town in North Africa. His father Patricius was a civil servant, who did not, until his final illness, share his wife Monica's strong and uncompromising Christian faith. Augustine does not seem to have had much respect for his father; most of the mentions of him in the *Confessions* are uncomplimentary. He was, however, grateful for the excellent education his father bought for him at a school at Madaura, twenty miles from his home. That classical education enabled sixteen-year-old Augustine to win a place in Carthage to study rhetoric.

In this chapter we see young Augustine just before he set out for Carthage. Of course, all the events are viewed from much later in his life. What we have is a middle-aged bishop's account of his experiences as a teen-ager. That accounts for the sudden little sermons, pointing out the errors and follies of the younger Augustine.

Already one or two traits in his character were emerging. Like many teen-agers, Augustine was embarrassed about his awakening sexuality. He did not appreciate his father's jokes about it, and even seemed to think that his mother's attitude was rather lax. Of course, we don't know what he thought about it at the time. But perhaps his persistent anxiety about sex, which caused him agony in later years, began in this adolescent period.

Another distinctive trait is his tender conscience. I don't think that it is simply the perspective of middle age that gives us this picture of a sixteen-year-old who went through agonies of guilt about a few mediocre pears stolen from a neighbor's garden. Probably most of his friends had forgotten about it by the end of the week. But here is Augustine, worrying about it twenty-seven years later.

From that experience, however, he drew some pertinent lessons, even for readers in the twentieth century.

1

Wrong Priorities and False Ambitions at Sixteen

When I was sixteen, my life came to a turning point. My friends could see I was in danger of falling into immorality, but, far from discouraging me or pointing me toward marriage as an alternative, they seemed to care only that I should develop my skills as an orator and become rich and famous.

My father was neither rich nor famous, but he was very generous with me and paid for me to go away to study in Carthage. I'm not criticizing him and I'm not ungrateful; many parents, much richer than he, did much less for their children. But I have to say that he never seemed to worry about my morals or my lack of Christian faith. Nothing seemed to matter so long as I became "a man of culture." An empty goal.

My father had, of course, noticed that I was no longer a child. All that seemed to mean to him was that I might soon provide him with grandchildren. He was proud of my new virility. In fact, I overheard him laughing about it with my mother —though he wasn't entirely sober at the time, I believe.

To be fair to him, he was only a novice believer,

still under instruction as a Christian. But my mother was a mature believer, and she could see the dangers very clearly. She knew I wasn't a true Christian at all and was worried that I would set my life on such a wrong course that I would find it very hard to turn back.

She often warned me, and what she said, I now realize, was the truth from God. Yet even she was not wholehearted in restraining me, partly, I think, because of my father's views, and partly because she also had high hopes of me. Not hopes about my spiritual life, but hopes of fame through learning. So both of them pushed me along the same academic path, my father because he took too little regard of the Lord, my mother because (I honestly believe) she thought my studies might one day bring me to know and receive him. Mixed motives and wrong priorities on their part. Ordinary lust on mine. It was a dangerous mixture, and it did its work.

2

Why Do We Sin?

When I was about sixteen my friends and I used to round off our evening's horseplay by going to a nearby garden where there was a pear tree loaded down with fruit. We would shake its branches and make off with enormous quantities of pears. Not that we ate them; often we fed them to the pigs. The appeal wasn't that rather indifferent fruit, but the sheer thrill of stealing them. What a picture of human sin.

It's useless denying the sinful component in many everyday things. Gold and silver are attractive to the eye. The touch of human flesh is warm and pleasant. Being praised or exercising power over others can give us a lot of satisfaction. And there is nothing intrinsically wrong with our human capacity for enjoyment.

But we are not entitled to obtain what brings us pleasure by ignoring You, O Lord, or breaking Your laws.

Sin arises when things that are a minor good are pursued as though they were the most important goals in life. If money or affection or power are sought in disproportionate, obsessive ways, then sin occurs. And that sin is magnified when, for these lesser goals, we fail to pursue the highest good and the finest goals.

So when we ask ourselves why, in a given situation, we committed a sin, the answer is usually one of two things. Either we wanted to obtain something we didn't have, or we feared losing something we had. Take murder, as an extreme example. A man kills another man. Wouldn't an absolutely typical reason be that he wanted that man's wife, or something else that he possessed, and was prepared to kill to get it? Or that he was afraid that the other man was about to deprive him of his wife, or of some valued possession or position?

I suppose one would have to add the motive of revenge too. But in general we would regard it as incredible that anyone would kill simply for the delight he found in killing. Yet the things we do kill for are hardly ever of the highest order of importance: God's honor, his truth, and his law. Mostly those things are connected with what we might call "creaturely pleasures": the beauty of silver and gold, honor and status in the world's eyes, the pleasure of the touch of flesh, the joy of human friendship and its possessive ties.

Those things do give pleasure, and some of them are good, in a secondary way (and can be fully and completely good, if the obtaining of them is within the Lord's will and according to his laws). But to pursue them for themselves is to commit a kind of spiritual fornication: to seek pleasure selfishly, self-indulgently, and apart from God.

Let's take some examples. Pride struggles to push us to the top of the heap. But the top of the heap is not vacant. God is there, high above all. Ambition drives us to seek power and glory—but the glory and the power are Yours, Lord. The promiscuous man or woman is looking desperately for some kind of love in return, but fails to see the love of God, offered freely and without condition.

Some people, on the other hand, seek simplicity

and innocence (though sometimes what they are really looking for is ignorance and stupidity). Yet nothing is more *simple,* in the word's real meaning, than the utter consistency of God, nor more *innocent* than the One whose every action is totally opposed to evil. The lazy person is looking for a kind of rest, I suppose, but true rest is found only in God. Others search restlessly for satisfaction in this or that sensual experience, but only "at his right hand" are there "pleasures forevermore." Truly our hearts are restless until they find their rest in You, O Lord. We may confuse being generous with being wasteful, but God, who is infinitely generous, wastes nothing. We long to possess things; God already possesses everything. We grieve because we lose things we have enjoyed. We forget that only in eternity can anything be ours forever.

In other words, sin comes when we take a perfectly natural desire or longing or ambition and try desperately to fulfil it without God. Not only is it sin, it is a perverse distortion of the image of the Creator in us. All these good things, and all our security, are rightly found only and completely in him.

3

A Double Mercy

How could anyone do what I did: enjoy something wrong simply and solely because it *was* wrong? I stole pears I didn't want, because I enjoyed the act of stealing. Thank You, Lord, for forgiving me all my evil actions.

And I thank You for Your mercy and grace that have kept me from far worse sin, because surely anyone who could sin on so slight a ground—not even wanting the consequences of the sin, but merely the pleasure of committing it—would have been capable of infinitely greater evil than the theft of a few tasteless pears? So I am grateful that You have forgiven me the sins I have actually committed, and also those which I would have committed but, because of Your help, I have not.

How can people have the nerve to claim that it is by their own moral strength that they have remained pure and innocent? Aren't they conscious of their inner weakness, of how frail they are in the face of temptation? In any case, the result of such self-confidence is that they are less grateful to You. They love You less, because they don't appreciate the extent of Your mercy. You do not simply forgive sinners, but deliver them from their sins. Both actions are expressions of Your mercy.

It is mercy to the one who does wrong, and also to the one who would have done wrong but for Your grace.

4

When Company Corrupts

On reflection, I would never have stolen those wretched pears if I had been on my own. It is true I enjoyed the thrill of the theft, but I enjoyed much more the excitement of the gang. I don't believe it would ever have occurred to me to steal the fruit but for the company I was in.

I'm not saying I am incapable of sinning on my own, but in that case there was no personal satisfaction or reward, and consequently no personal motivation. As I have said, I didn't even like the pears.

So what was it about the company that made the action desirable? It wasn't that I was particularly fond of my companions or especially enjoyed their company. But doing it together made it fun. We laughed a lot, and imagined what the owner would say when he found out what had happened. We boasted together about the way we'd outwitted him and gotten away with it.

Those things don't happen to us on our own. We don't laugh much on our own, or boast much on our own. But when young men get together, what is at first just a bit of fun easily turns into something cruel, greedy, or vicious. There's no motive or reason for it, often enough, beyond a fear of being different, of standing out, or being thought cowardly. We are ashamed that we aren't shameless.

Again, what a picture of fallen human nature, that friendship and company, which are gifts of God, can be so easily perverted. So friendship itself can seduce us and lead us astray.

But the person who keeps company with You, Lord, finds joy. In Your fellowship there is satisfaction, security, and happiness. Apart from it, as I discovered in those dark and distant days, life is a miserable wasteland.

CHAPTER TWO

Wrestling
with Truth

This chapter covers an important period in Augustine's life, his years as a student in Carthage. There, through the writings of Cicero, he learned that the pursuit of wisdom is more important than prestige or material wealth. That idea never left him, and in fact became the basis of a sincere search for truth that lasted all his life.

But also in Carthage, and when he was only seventeen, Augustine took a lover. A year later, the woman bore him a son, Adeodatus. From that time on—and although at times he despised himself for it—he found it impossible to live without a consort or mistress. He was loyal to his first lover for fifteen years, though later (when he was committed to a wife) he did take another mistress, as we shall see. This "weakness," as he saw it, was a constant burden to him and eventually was the chief barrier to his conversion.

Augustine spent a short time as a teacher in his home town, where the death of a close friend made a deep impression on him. Then, appointed to an excellent post in Rome, he spent several eventful years there with a group of like-minded friends. They all saw themselves as rather intellectual "seekers after the truth," but (as Augustine put it) they "did not see that their intelligence itself was a gift of God."

Manichaeism, which Augustine followed for many years, was a corruption of Christianity that rejected any notion of God being found in material or human form. Consequently, Augustine found the incarnation, with its picture of God taking human form in Jesus, the Word "becoming flesh," totally unacceptable. Manichaeism was only one of a number of heresies that had taken root at that time, and when Monica prayed that Augustine would find his home in the "Catholic" church she meant, of course, the Christian group that had remained faithful to the teaching of the apostles, the orthodox, biblical church that had stood firm against all kinds of strange and transitory ideas.

At the end of the chapter we see Augustine taking a big step: he turned from Manichaeism.

Then, in another important new job, in Milan, he came under the influence of Bishop Ambrose and decided to begin a course of instruction in the Christian faith.

5

The Importance of Truth

When I was studying rhetoric at Carthage I came across a book by the Greek philosopher Cicero. I read it because I'd been told that his language was elegant and his arguments persuasive, and those were skills I desperately wanted to acquire. What I hadn't expected was the effect that Cicero's book would have on me. Without exaggeration I can say that it changed my whole attitude toward life.

The book was called *Hortensius,* and it was really a call to its readers to love wisdom, or what the Greeks called "philosophy." The effect it had on me was dramatic, inciting desires I had never had before. I saw that eloquence—*how* you say something—is much less important than truth—*what* you say. In other words, manner is secondary to matter.

Cicero created in me a great longing to turn from material and worldly things to the pursuit of wisdom. That Greek word *philosophy* speaks of the love of wisdom, and I was stirred up, even inflamed, not toward this or that set of beliefs, but to loving, seeking, finding, and holding onto wisdom itself, whatever wisdom might be.

I was nineteen at the time and was supported financially by my mother, my father having died two years before. She was buying for me the art of eloquence, but Cicero persuaded me that there was something more important than style. At that time I began to rise from the depths into which I had sunk. I didn't know the letters of Paul, or any of the Scriptures, with their warnings against being deceived by false philosophy "according to human traditions," but Cicero warned against those who gloss over immorality with smooth and high-sounding arguments to which they give the name of philosophy.

Only one thing made me cautious about following Cicero's arguments totally: he never mentioned the name of Christ. Although I was not a believer, I had drunk in that name with my mother's milk. So deeply was it implanted in my thinking that I could never be completely satisfied with any argument, no matter how learned or eloquent, that omitted giving Christ a place in its discussion.

So, as a direct result of reading a pagan philosopher, I resolved to turn to the Bible to see what kind of book it was and what it could contribute to my search for wisdom. I came to it at that time, however, with too much pride. The Bible is a book for those who come to it humbly, bowing before its sublime mysteries. I came to it as a critic, and soon concluded that it was not worthy to be compared with Cicero for grandeur of language or ideas.

I did not know then that the Scriptures do not yield their mysteries to proud human eyes. My pride refused to humble myself before them. I did not realize that the Scriptures grow with the spiritual baby inch by inch, and proceed step by step. Simple truths for the simple, profound truths for the mature. I was sure I was mature already, and so I missed the point completely.

6

A Mother's Dream

When I was a young man, rejecting my mother's faith and disappointing her prayers, the Lord sent her a remarkable vision. It came at a time when she was desperately worried about me; she wept for me more bitterly than a mother who had lost her only son through death. And, in her view, I *was* dead—dead in unbelief, spiritually dead. As a result, she could not bring herself to have me in the house or at the family table. She found my blasphemies and cynicism unbearable.

Then, in a dream, came this vision. She saw

herself standing on a wooden rostrum. A young man—an angel, perhaps—approached her. She was overwhelmed with anxiety about me; he looked cheerful and positive. He asked her what was wrong, and she explained that she was worried about the way I was destroying my life by rejecting God.

The young man's reply surprised her. He suggested, as an antidote to her anxiety, that she should turn round and observe where her son was standing. She did, and was astonished to discover that I was beside her on the rostrum. The "angel" pointed out that where she was, I was too. She took his words as tremendous reassurance, direct from God, that he had heard her prayers for me, and all would eventually be well.

I believe it was also from God that she was given an answer to my own rather cynical interpretation of her dream. I suggested that what it meant was that one day she would have the same religion as I (whatever that might be). "No," she immediately countered, "I wasn't told, 'where he is, you will be,' but 'where you are, he will be.' "

That answer impressed me deeply at the time, and I often recalled it during the following nine years when I continued to grope my way through the darkness of error and unbelief. All that while, this devout and faithful woman continued to pray for me, more optimistically, but still with a great deal of grief and tears for the life I continued to lead. But her prayers *were* answered, and one day, after nine years of stubborn rebellion, I did indeed stand where she stood.

7

Breaking the Hold of Astrology

During the time when I was studying rhetoric, I entered a competition for a dramatic poem. Just before the contest I got a message from a medium, asking me what I would pay him if he arranged for me to win. As it happened, I detested the occult and especially the idea of animals being sacrificed in order to procure the favor of the gods.

So I wrote back to him saying that if the prize were made of solid gold, and immortal, I wouldn't agree to a single fly losing its life if that were the price of my victory. I did not take this stand on any Christian ground, of course. Far from it, because in other respects I was as superstitious as the occultists.

That was especially true of my addiction to astrology. I felt that it was somehow better, because it did not involve sacrifices or prayers to the spirits. What I did not see was how astrology also strikes at the roots of human responsibility. It says, in effect, "It wasn't my fault; it was decided by the stars," or "Venus caused it, or Saturn or Mars—not my weakness or sin." It left me, mere flesh and blood and proud corruption, without sin. The Creator of sky and stars was to be blamed for whatever I did. And who is that Creator but our God, the center and source of justice?

At about that time, however, I met a doctor, Vindicianus, whom I came to admire. He was pro-consul at the time, and in the course of his duties he had to award me a prize, which he did by placing a garland on my head. Certainly my head *needed* a doctor's attention, though he did not know it at the time.

Anyway, I was drawn to this elderly man, whom God used to draw me away from self-destruction. He was a marvelous talker. He did not waste words, but had a lively common sense that balanced the serious and the lighthearted perfectly.

When he soon discovered my addiction to the stars, his advice was to throw away the birth charts and predictions. After all, he pointed out, I had better things to do with my time than waste it on such frivolity.

He told me about his own experience. As a young man he had intended to make astrology his profession. He had studied Hippocrates, which made the "science" of astrology fairly easy to master. Later, however, he rejected it completely and took up medicine. His reason was simple. He liked to think of himself as an honest man and as such he could not bring himself to make money by deception. And deception was what he had discovered astrology to be. In his words, it was "utterly false."

His advice to me was to abandon it. "After all," he argued, "rhetoric is your profession, and you are well able to make your living at it. You don't have to indulge in this deceitful practice; it's just a hobby to you. So listen to someone who did study it seriously and made his living at it, and give it up."

I was impressed by his concern, but wanted to know why, if it was such falsehood, it often managed to produce accurate predictions. He suggested that it was pure chance, as irrational as opening a book of poetry and putting your finger on a line at random to find guidance for business or personal affairs. Sometimes, of course, the poetic line seems applicable, simply on the law of averages. But it is demonstrably chance, because the poet had no intention of giving such guidance.

Vindicianus did not convince me at the time. I was more impressed by all the famous and brilliant men who consulted the stars. I found it hard to believe that the whole art was based on chance. But he had sowed the seeds of doubt in my mind.

Some time later I finally became convinced that Vindicianus, and another friend, Nebridius, who were both so skeptical of the validity of astrology, were right. The circumstances in which I came to that conclusion were somewhat strange.

I had a close friend, Firminus, who came to me

for help. He was hoping for promotion in his business and wanted to know how I read the stars in this matter. Like me, he was trained in liberal studies and rhetoric, and also like me he was fascinated by astrology but becoming slightly skeptical about it.

I agreed to read the stars for him, but remarked that I was no longer sure that it was a valid thing to do. He then told me about a remarkable incident involving his father.

Many years before, his father and a friend were serious students of astrology. They were so serious, in fact, that they even made a practice of being present at the birth of any creature in their household in order to make a note of the exact time and compare it with the astrological charts.

When Firminus's mother was pregnant, this friend of his father reported that the wife of one of his slaves was also pregnant. They decided to follow these two births with meticulous attention, to compare the two birth charts.

As it happened, the two babies were born at exactly the same time, though in different households, of course. Both were boys, and one of them was named Firminus (who became my friend). But he was aware that miles away in another city was a young slave of exactly the same age, with the same birth chart, who was living a very different life.

That fact bothered Firminus. Why, if they both had the same birth sign and exactly the same astrological chart, should their lives have been so different? He was a wealthy, cultured, successful man of affairs; the other was still a slave, poor, uneducated, and struggling to provide for himself and his family.

But, as I pointed out to him, the situation was more complicated. Here we were, studying the stars to see whether Firminus was destined to achieve the promotion he wanted. But why, if the stars determined that the job should be his, did not exactly the same conjunction determine that the young slave should get it? If there was anything rational about astrology, these two men should have led identical lives, whereas in fact their lives were totally different.

The consequence was obvious. As I tried to read the stars for Firminus, I could either give him a different reading from the slave (bearing in mind his circumstances) or, being true to the art, give both an identical reading, which might prove true for Firminus but could not be true for the slave.

That led me also to think of twins, necessarily born under the same constellation, and especially of Esau and Jacob, in the book of Genesis, who were such different characters and had such different destinies. We concluded that the whole thing was nonsense.

Surely, Lord, the truth is in Your hands alone. No one should say "What will happen?" In your unfathomable wisdom You determine the outcome of events, the destinies of each individual.

8

Tears of Bitterness

About the time I began to work as a teacher in my home town, I gained the closest friend I have ever had. We had known each other since childhood, right through school and university. We studied together and played together, enjoying one other's company and being challenged by the other's ideas and attitudes.

Although my friend had been a Christian from childhood, I set out to divert him from his faith and succeeded, much to my satisfaction. We were, it has to be said, perfectly happy together in our unbelief. However—such are the ways of God— our friendship was suddenly tested. He picked up an infection, and fever spread through his body until he became unconscious. The doctors said he was beyond recovery.

At that point, and without his consent, of course, he was baptized. His relatives presumed that he would have wished to be baptized in the faith of his youth. To me it seemed a meaningless gesture. I had won his mind over to unbelief, so what difference could it make putting water on his body?

Yet, oddly enough, it *did* make a difference. He came out of the coma and seemed to be completely

well again, well enough at least for us to discuss
what had happened and his feelings about it. As
soon as I got the chance to speak to him, I began
pouring scorn on this superstitious business of his
baptism, assuming he would agree. But much to
my surprise he told me to stop talking like that if
I wanted to remain his friend. So I stopped, assuming that when he was fully recovered I would have
little trouble in persuading him what nonsense
the whole thing had been.

However, that was not to be. Within a few days
the fever returned more powerfully than ever, and
he died.

I was surprised at my reaction. My heart was
darkened, and everything I saw seemed to exhibit
the dark face of death. All the things we had enjoyed together became a kind of torment, now
that he was not there to share them. I had no
grounds to tell myself to "hope in God." My only
relief was in tears, which came constantly from
the heart of my being. They were tears of bitterness, but they were also, I suppose, a kind of plea
or prayer for help.

Everything reminded me of him: the places we
walked in, the sports arena, concerts, books,
meals, even the company of women. I kept coming
back to this desperate sense of loss. I could not
escape from myself, but did the next best thing.
I moved from Tagaste to Carthage. Then, as inevitably happens, time worked its slow but certain healing, rolling idly around my senses and

working subtly on my thinking.

As my grief passed, I was able to look back at the experience. Why had it hurt so much? Surely because I had poured my affection into a bed of sand, loving a person who was going to die some-day as if he had been immortal. What I have learned later, however, is even more important: The happy man is the one who loves You, O Lord, You who are immortal and unchangeable, and then loves his friend only *in* You, and loves his enemy *for* You.

9

God of Beauty

Whichever way the human heart turns, except to-ward You, O Lord, it is wedded to pain. That is true even when it fastens on the most beautiful things You have made, tree or flower, leaf or bud. All of those things have both a spring and a fall: a spring, when they hasten toward perfection, and a fall, when they wither and die. It is their nature, of course, to do so, as parts of the created nature.

What folly, then, to attach our affection to any creature, subject to this law of death. I can praise God for their beauty, but must recognize that they all hasten toward oblivion. Indeed, those that more speedily bloom to perfection more speedily cease to be. It is the way of the world, the endless succession of its parts, the one making way for its successor.

"But do I ever depart?" asks the Word of God. The Lord does not abandon what he has made, but is present within it, so that when we find delight in it we are really finding delight in him. On that foundation we can build, loving his creatures, but (best of all) loving him in his creatures.

Indeed, our one true Life, the Son of God, came down to this planet to bear our death, the death of a creature, but through the power of life within him conquered it. He calls us with a voice of thunder to come back to him. And though he has returned to heaven, yet still we can find him within our hearts, present within the life he has made, and giving it new life.

10

The Eternal Wisdom

When I was just twenty it gave me great satisfaction that I managed to read, and understand, the *Ten Categories* of Aristotle without a teacher. I would mention the book at every opportunity, slipping the title in with a touch almost of awe, smiling to myself when my lecturers would comment how difficult it had been for them to master it.

And much good it did me! Indeed, it was harmful, because it encouraged me to think of You, O Lord, as if You were part of what You had made, instead of being its essence and origin. Sadly, I had my back toward the light and my eyes fixed on the darkness. I could understand without difficulty logic, rhetoric, geometry, music, and arithmetic, but I did not see that my intelligence itself was a gift of God and that all the true things I learned came from him, their source.

What advantage was it to me that I had a nimble wit when all the while I turned from good and clung to evil? Little did I realize then, how much better off were all those (as I saw then) "simple" souls who lacked my native intelligence but put their trust in God and sheltered safely within the nest of his church.

11

A Mother Prays

About that time I was desperately ill, almost, as we say, "at death's door." Had I died, I would surely have gone to hell, my sins unforgiven because unrepented, and unrepented because I could not see how Christ could have borne my sins in his body, since I did not really believe that he *had* a body. I was influenced by the sect of the Manichees, and thought like them of Christ as having a spiritual or angelic kind of body rather than human flesh and blood.

My mother knew nothing of my beliefs, nor for that matter of my illness, but as always she was praying for me in my absence: my absence from home, and my absence from the church to which she was devotedly attached. Looking back, I cannot believe that God could have ignored or rejected her prayers, which were as painful and costly as they struggled from her lips as the childbirth must have been that brought me into the world from her body. How could God have turned a deaf ear to that contrite and humble widow, who was so generous to others, who served the church so modestly, who came every day to the eucharist, and twice every day into the church to pray and to listen to his voice? How could God have closed his eyes to her tears, the tears with which she begged him not for gold or silver, nor for fleeting earthly fame, but simply for her wayward son's salvation?

So in answer to her unspoken prayers, the Lord healed me and raised me up. There in Rome, surrounded by my friends with their strange beliefs, God reached out and touched me. But I was unmoved. My pride was such that I clung to the notion of my own sinlessness. Following the Manichean beliefs, I excused myself of my sins on the grounds that it was not I who sinned, but the principle of evil physically present in me— whereas in truth I am a unity, and it was my own sinful disobedience that created this inner conflict. But at the time, that was something I could not accept. It would have destroyed my self-esteem.

So my recovery from illness did not immediately bring me closer to God. I was, however, taken by the idea, commonly held by intellectuals in Rome, that we should doubt and question everything, because no ultimate truth can ever be comprehended by human beings. At the same time I did not see all the implications of such an outlook. For instance, my landlord was totally devoted to the incredible stories of which the Manichean books were full, but I did not think to warn him to approach them with more skepticism. But I was becoming more skeptical of them myself, or at any rate I did not defend them as ardently as I had formerly.

Sadly, I was completely unwilling to turn to the church for answers, despairing of finding truth in the Christian faith from which my friends had diverted me, and which taught the doctrine (one I found disgusting) that God himself was Spirit but had taken flesh and blood in his Son. Surely, I felt, that would mean that Jesus, born in the flesh, would also have been defiled by the flesh. The very idea repelled me. But at least I was think-

ing and questioning. And my mother, God bless
her, was praying.

An Important Decision

So I was in a bit of a quandry. I could see, increasingly, that the ideas of the Manichees were weak.
They simply had no answer to certain passages
of Scripture that Christian friends pointed out to
me. They were even reduced to arguing that the
New Testament had been falsified by someone
(they never said who) who wanted to combine
the Jewish law with the gospel. Mind you, they
could not produce the original, uncorrupted version.

I still could not accept the idea of a spiritual
entity having a physical substance, which meant
that I continued to reject the idea of Jesus as both
man and God. That kind of conflict went on in
my mind all the time that I was teaching rhetoric
in Rome.

Eventually I heard of a wonderful post in Milan,
one I knew I would enjoy. Evidently the Prefect
of the city of Rome was asked to nominate a Master
of Rhetoric for Milan, to be paid out of public
funds. Some of my Manichean friends were very

influential, got me nominated, and paid for me to travel to Milan to take up the post.

As it happened, the job required my working closely with the bishop of Milan, Ambrose, someone I had heard a lot about and respected because of his outstanding ability as an orator. He was courteous and friendly to me, in a fatherly sort of way, and I soon became very attached to him—not, sadly, at that time to his doctrine, which I now know to have been the true teaching of the Bible, but to him as a man and a scholar.

I listened to him preaching with intense pleasure, even though I rejected the heart of his message, which was salvation. "Salvation is far from sinners," of course, and that is what I was then—though, little by little, and largely unaware of it, I did draw closer each day to that salvation of which he preached.

What I began to learn from Ambrose was that the Christian faith could be defended intellectually. It was not, as I had previously thought, intrinsically absurd. I particularly valued the wonderful way in which he explained, one after another, many of the difficult passages in the Old Testament. It was especially impressive to me because I knew the passages well, as far as the actual words went. But because I was spiritually dead I had never been able to understand them. That was a blow to my pride, I suppose, but it was something I had to learn.

So there I was, torn between one set of beliefs,

those of the Manichees, which I now profoundly doubted, and another set, those of the Christians, which I had begun to admire but which had for me one impossible difficulty. If I could once conceive of a *spiritual substance*, then the last foothold of the Manichees in my mind would be captured.

I made an important decision. I would leave the sect of the Manichees, because I no longer shared their beliefs. I would become a catechumen, undergoing instruction in the Christian faith, until such time as some certainty of truth came to me. Needless to say, my mother was delighted.

CHAPTER THREE

Marking Time
in Milan

At this time, Augustine's mother joined him in Milan. It is impossible to exaggerate the influence this amazing woman had on her brilliant son. Almost equally important was the influence of Ambrose, whose biblical preaching continued to impress Augustine, especially giving him new respect for the Old Testament.

Mental and moral battles continued to rage inside him, however. The intellectuals in Rome had influenced him to be skeptical about the idea of proving, and hence believing, *anything*. Having abandoned the dogmas of the Manichees, he was reluctant simply to pick up another set of propositions, the "Catholic" ones. So he wavered between skepticism and faith, remaining a kind of permanent seeker.

Possibly more important than those intellectual problems, however, was the great moral issue that nagged away at his conscience. He knew that his life did not match his self-image as a seeker after spiritual truth. On the other hand, his pleasure in self-indulgence was gradually slipping away. He found himself neither a confident saint nor a satisfied sinner.

Something would have to change.

13

Accepting Correction

My mother joined me in Milan, so I was able to tell her that I had rejected false doctrine (which she had for a long while pleaded with me to do) but had not yet turned to the faith she held so devoutly. I know she was pleased, but she was wise enough not to make a big thing of it. It was simply that she had faith that what You, Lord, had promised would come about—not just that I would be freed from falsehood, but that I would be delivered into the hands of truth. All she said to me was that she "surely hoped in Christ that she would see me a faithful Catholic before she passed from this life."

Of course, she said a great deal more to the Lord. I know she prayed even more fervently for my conversion and went eagerly to the church to hear Bishop Ambrose preach. She had come to admire him too, as the "angel of God" whom God had used to bring me to my present open, if wavering, state of mind as a catechumen.

During those days in Milan my mother had an experience that showed me yet again what an amazing woman she was.

In North Africa many of the Christians had a custom, which my mother shared in enthusiastically, of taking cakes, bread, and wine to the shrines of saintly Christians who had died, and there eating and drinking with anyone else who happened to be visiting the tombs. It was seen as a mark of respect and fellowship with those who had died in Christ.

When she came to Milan she decided to honor the shrines of the saints in the same way, and set off with her little basket containing the cakes, bread, and wine. At the gate of the cemetery she was stopped by the doorkeeper, who explained that Bishop Ambrose had forbidden the custom. My mother was surprised, of course, but when she heard the bishop's reasons she quietly accepted his decision. He felt that there was danger of the custom's becoming a disorderly social event, with rather too much drinking. Also, more seriously, the practice had pagan elements in it.

I was impressed by the way my mother was prepared to abandon a custom that had meant so much to her—and abandon it not reluctantly but gladly, once the arguments against it were explained to her. So rather than taking a basket of food to the tombs of the saints she took just her heart, with its holy longings and prayers, and gave the food to the poor instead.

It was an object lesson to me in true humility: the readiness of really mature persons to accept correction, and change not only their mind but their practice. Her response impressed Ambrose too. When we met he broke into praising her, congratulating me on having such a mother. What a pity that *she* had such a son, who could not at that time bring himself to find that way of life and faith that meant so much to her.

14

My Problems with Proof

I would have loved to discuss all my intellectual and spiritual problems with Bishop Ambrose: he seemed to be the kind of happy man one could talk to. But, regrettably, he was never free. Crowds of people surrounded him all the time, and when he *was* alone he was immersed in study. He never isolated himself, his door was never shut, and there was no secretary to keep people away. But I realized he was entirely occupied with his ministry and with the many people who already depended on him. I longed to ask him what gave him his sense of serenity, how he coped with celibacy (something that was quite inconceivable to me), what his hopes and temptations were, what joy he found in the sacrament, where he found strength to cope with problems, opponents, and disappointments. But I could not, although I spent a lot of time with him. Frankly, the tumult of my mind would have required hours, even days, of his time, and that was not possible.

Still, I heard him preaching every Sunday, and whatever else I made of his words, at least he convinced me of this, that those who scoffed at the Scriptures were totally wrong.

He also helped me by showing that many beliefs held by Christians which I had found incredible or irrational were in fact perversions of true Christian doctrine. One of them, he explained, was an idea held by many of my Christian friends—that, because "God made man in his own image," God also has a bodily form. It was such a relief to find that all the time I had thought I was opposing the true faith I was in fact opposing only a distortion of it.

Mind you, the problem remained. If (as Am-

brose said and the Scriptures taught) God is Spirit,
and is in no way to be thought of as confined to
a human body, how could it be that man, who
from head to foot is confined to a particular place,
is made "in his image"? At the time I could see
no answer. But at least I could now appreciate this
vision of God, the Creator of all things, filling all
things, and not in any way contracted or squeezed
into any space or place, or limited in any way by
material being. That vision alone moved me to the
extent that I began to believe that the truth (could
I but find it) lay in the church's teachings.

My trouble was that I could not firmly assent
to anything unless I could prove it. I wanted to
be certain even of invisible things, as sure of the
things of faith as I was that seven and three make
ten.

I suppose, having found that the beliefs of the
Manichees, to which I had long assented, were
false, I was reluctant to be caught again. I was like
a person who, having been treated by an imcom-
petent doctor, is reluctant to trust himself even to
a good one afterward. I could be healed only by
believing. But believing was the one thing I
couldn't do.

15

No Pleasure in Sin

My career was going well, but, in the way things are, that only increased the pressure on me. I wanted honor, wealth, and good sex, but God mocked my ambitions. He made sure that none of those things gave me any pleasure. If he could not (without overriding my free will) prevent my sinning, he could and did prevent my enjoying it.

I was very flattered to be invited to give an oration in praise of the emperor. On the day it was to be given I was inwardly in turmoil, knowing that I was to utter many flattering untruths about him, and be applauded by people who knew that untruths were what they were.

As I walked to the gathering through the streets of Milan, I noticed a poor beggar. He was, I'm pretty sure, half drunk; he was certainly merry. And that was what struck me. I, on my way to this important occasion, was miserable and anxious. He, with nothing to do and no one to impress, was serenely happy.

I commented on this to my companions, pointing out how all our complex ambitions and desires served only to put burdens on us. We strove to be happy, contented, and successful, but we ended up burdened and unhappy. The beggar sought nothing, really, but a few cents-worth of wine, and out of that he contrived a kind of satisfaction.

Well, they pointed out, what he had was not true joy. It was bogus. So was mine, I replied—in fact, more bogus than his. Of course I would rather be in my shoes than his, but even that seemed to me an irrational choice. I was cleverer than he was, true, but he was happier than I was.

Still, my friends said, the important thing is not joy, but the grounds of that joy. The beggar's joy came from alcohol; mine, they claimed, came from a noble desire for glory. But what glory? My inner self protested. Certainly no true and noble glory, nor the glory of God. If the beggar's joy was not true joy, then equally my glory was not true glory. He got his wine by wishing passersby good luck, while I got my "glory" from pride based on flattery. He would sleep off his drunkenness that night. I would carry my guilt to bed with me—yes, and wake up with it too.

I kept arguing with my friends like that. Of course, they didn't agree, but actually they proved my point by trying to assuage my anxiety with flattery. But it would not be assuaged. My experience at that time, as I resisted God's insistent invitation to me, was the awful realization that I was on a self-destructive course. It made me miserable to admit it. Worse, when for a brief while I found something enjoyable and satisfying, I still could not enjoy it. Every time I stretched out my hand for it, it flew away.

CHAPTER FOUR

Friendship
with Alipius

Augustine's closest friend during his twenties was
Alipius, a young man who was at first his pupil
in Tagaste and Carthage, was subsequently with
him in Rome, and then in Milan. He was several
years younger than Augustine, but the older man
greatly admired his sincerity, judgment, and integ-
rity.

Together they argued out the rights and wrongs
of various philosophies of life. With a larger group
of about ten friends they pursued their search for
the truth. But it was Alipius who shared some of
Augustine's most important experiences, in-

cluding the occasion of his conversion.

Augustine occasionally speaks of Alipius with hindsight, mentioning how qualities that were latent or emerging in him as a young man became important in his later life. In fact, the career of Alipius followed Augustine's quite closely. He also was ordained a presbyter, and ended up, appropriately, as bishop of their home town, Tagaste.

16

Obsession with Sport

Among the friends I lived with, one of my favorites was a young man called Alipius. He came from the same town, where his parents were leading figures. Because he was younger than I, several times found myself being his teacher, first in our home town, and later in Carthage. He openly admired what he saw as my learning and easy disposition; and I admired his promise, both of high moral standards and intelligence.

When he came to Carthage where I was teaching rhetoric, he did not become my pupil at first, because of some antagonism between his father and me. What he did become, sadly, was addicted to sport.

The sport in question was the arena, where

chariot racing and various kinds of violent hand-to-hand combats drew enormous crowds of screaming spectators. It was thoroughly degrading and brutalizing, but I felt I had no right to intervene where Alipius was concerned. I was not his teacher and did not consider myself then to be his friend, assuming he held the same opinion of me as his father. In fact he did not, but I was not aware of that at the time.

Eventually, however, he began to look in on my lecture and wave a greeting. For my part I was reluctant to say anything about what I saw as his foolish obsession with the games, but in a strange way I was used (by God, I later came to believe) to make him reconsider his addiction.

I was talking about a piece of literature, and an illustration from the arena came into my mind to help explain some point. Without any intention of influencing Alipius, I slipped in a derogatory remark about people who were obsessed with the games. Amazingly, he took this to heart and assumed I had directed it specifically at him. Instead of reacting angrily, as many would have done, he appreciated what he saw as my helpful and friendly warning. As a result, and immediately, he stopped going to the arena and cleared his mind of all the filth associated with those sports.

What was more, with his father's permission, he became my pupil and began to share the devotion I had at that time to the teaching of the Manichees. That continued until he went to Rome—

before the time I was there—to study law.

In Rome, regrettably, he had another encounter with the games. The great arenas like the Colosseum drew enormous crowds, people who went there to indulge their lust for blood as the gladiators hacked each other to death. Alipius, in line with his decision at Carthage, kept well away. Then one evening some friends called on him after supper and with mock violence threatened to carry him off by force to the arena with them.

His reaction was typical: He had determined not to go, and his mind was set against it. However, they pleaded and cajoled and half dragged him out of the house, so that in the end he agreed to go, but told them he would sit in the arena with his eyes shut and his mind closed to the obscenities going on below him in the stadium.

"You may think I am physically present with you," he said, "but actually I shall be absent—and that will defeat your plan to get me to that evil event." Those were brave words, but also, as it turned out, overconfident ones.

Alipius and his friends arrived at the ground, where the crowd was already in a great state of excitement, and with difficulty found seats. As he had said he would, Alipius closed his eyes and tried to shut out of his imagination all the noises and excitement around him.

For a while all went well. Then, at the end of a savage fight, a contestant was hacked down with the sword, and the crowd leapt to their feet in a hideous howl of approval. Alipius couldn't resist opening his eyes to see what had happened, "determined to oppose it and despise it," as he claimed afterward. But what he saw affected him spiritually as certainly as it had slain the gladiator.

His mistake, as he realized later, was to have trusted in his own strength to overcome temptation. Now, he could not resist the sight. He was on his feet with the others, baying for blood. He no longer was the decent young man who had high moral beliefs and who despised the decadence and savagery of the arena. Rather, he was a brute, just like the rest, staring and shouting and enjoying the vicious spectacle. What was worse, after that, he went back time and again and persuaded others to go with him.

What he did not know then, of course, was that the Lord would one day call him to the Christian ministry, to preside at the sacrament and care for Christ's flock. Nor did he know that many years later God would draw him away from all these present follies with a strong and merciful hand, teaching him to trust not in himself but in the Lord.

17

Another Painful Experience

That experience of Alipius in the arena was equaled by another one that happened to him in Carthage, at the time when I was his teacher. Both events, as it happened, were stored away in his memory, and had their value later in life, but right then they were very painful.

One day in Carthage he was strolling through the marketplace at midday, rehearsing aloud something he was trying to learn, and carrying his tablets and stylus. Unknown to him, another young student was also in the marketplace, with less innocent motives. He had brought an axe with him, and by climbing onto the roof of a silversmith's booth intended to hack off some of the lead gratings up there and steal them.

Not surprisingly, the noise of an axe on lead alerted the silversmiths down below, who came outside to see what was going on. The thief realized his danger and scrambled away, leaving his axe on the ground near the booth.

Alipius heard all the commotion and strolled over to see what it was all about. He noticed the thief making off (though he did not know what he had done), and then came across the axe lying on the ground, which he picked up. At that moment the silversmiths showed up and saw Alipius standing there with the incriminating instrument in his hand. Putting two and two together, and despite his protests, they dragged him off to the magistrates, carrying with them the axe as evidence.

His fate would certainly have been a prison sentence, or perhaps a public flogging, had not a certain distinguished architect crossed their path. The silversmiths were pleased to see him, to tell him what had happened, but so was Alipius, who had met him several times in the home of a mutual friend, a senator. The architect took Alipius aside and asked him for his side of the story. Unlike the crowd, he was aware of what had really taken place, and led them, with Alipius, to the house of the prime suspect. At the door of the building was a young slave-boy, too young, the architect guessed, to realize the implication of the question, "Whose axe is this?"

"Ours," said the boy immediately, and that led them to his master, who eventually confessed, much to the relief of Alipius. He went home a wiser young man than he had left it. He had learned, too, something that would stand him in good stead many years later when the Lord called him to be a judge and examiner of many causes in the church. Things are not always what they seem.

18

The Intellectual Quest

Alipius was one of a small group of friends, about ten in number, who came together in Milan as students of the law. Actually I had met him in Rome, and he had come with me to Milan.

I admired many of his qualities, but perhaps most of all I admired his single-minded honesty. Bribery was rife in the courts there, where he sat as assessor to the magistrates, and the pressure upon him was intense. But he had always despised the giving and receiving of bribes. Indeed, in Rome he had fallen foul of a prominent and powerful senator who offered him a bribe to ease some legal question. When Alipius refused, the man was incensed. He tried threats, but was rebuffed. Then he tried to influence the judge, in whose court Alipius was the assessor. But Alipius threatened to quit the court (and say why) if the judgment went in favor of the senator. The judge consequently had to rule against him, as the law required, but he laid the blame for the judgment on Alipius, who did not seem at all perturbed at the possible damage to his career.

To set the record straight, however, Alipius might have given way to the temptation to dishonesty over a much more trivial matter. He loved

books and study, and once when he was offered
the chance to buy pirated copies of some valuable
manuscripts at a very good price he was at first
inclined to accept. It was a common enough practice.

But he thought it over carefully, as he always
did, and decided not to compromise his principles
over a thing like that. It was a simple example of
the saying of Jesus, "He who is faithful in little is
faithful also in much." There is really no such thing
as a "little" dishonesty, and Alipius, better than
any of us, knew that.

Yet he who was so clear-cut on moral issues
hesitated over the biggest question of all. What
should be the guiding principle of his life? In that
he was in exactly the same situation as I and the
other members of our small circle. We claimed we
were untiring in our search for truth and wisdom,
but we never seemed to find them.

Three of us—the third was Nebridius—made,
I have to say, a particularly big show of that search.
We did a lot of sighing and heart-searching, constantly asking questions of each other, debating
far into the night, waiting at any moment for some
blinding flash of light to make it all clear.

Our social life and worldly activities went on,
of course. After all, we were men of the world. I
had my lover, and they had other pleasures to
pursue. *But those things gave no pleasure to any of
us.* All we gained from them was bitterness, and
all we could see ahead was darkness.

"How long will life go on like this?" we asked each other desperately. Yet it never occurred to us to stop doing the things that contradicted our search for truth—or that a connection might exist between our present life-style and the fact that the truly good life which we said we wanted never actually seemed to arrive.

For myself, I began to despair of ever finding the answer. My search had begun when I was nineteen, and I was now thirty and no nearer the truth, it seemed. Still, I rationalized the situation to myself. "Tomorrow," I would say, "the truth will appear plainly, and I shall accept it." Or, "Faustus, the great Manichean leader, will soon be in Milan, and he will clear up my difficulties." Or, less hopefully, "Is it perhaps true, as many intellectuals argue, that no certainty is possible in such matters, and the search for it is fruitless? Should I abandon the search?" Or, more hopefully, "I know what I will do. I have already seen that what the Bible teaches is not absurd. I've committed myself to Christian instruction. Surely I should just set my feet back on the path my parents put me on until such time as the truth becomes clear to me."

But even that excellent intention was contradicted by my actions. Like so many people, I enjoyed asking questions and posing as a seeker after truth, but I was pretty reluctant to give that great search the time and effort it really needed.

For instance, I had determined to do my academic work in the morning and spend the rest of the day in pursuit of spiritual truth. Fine. But then I began to ask myself, "When shall I have time for my friends?" or "When do I get to prepare my lectures?" or "When do I relax?"

I could see, in my moments of self-awareness, where all this was leading me, but I seemed powerless to change my ways. I knew that the hour of death was uncertain for me, as for everyone, and that to neglect or delay the serious search for truth on such trivial pretexts as parties, leisure, or even preparing lectures was stupid. Logic alone should have told me that the *first* priority was to find God and eternal life, before one became caught up in secondary questions.

But logic didn't. It told me that ambition was honorable. That to become, perhaps, a governor would bring great pleasure and satisfaction. That to be married, preferably to a wealthy wife, would ease at least two problems in life—sex and money. Those, I thought, were the modest limits of my desires. When I had achieved them, I would seriously seek the truth.

While I argued to and fro in that way, with myself and with my friends, time continued to slip past. I can see now that although I desperately wanted to be happy and fulfilled, I was afraid to seek the happy life in the one place where it could be found, which in my heart of hearts I knew. So

I fled from the truth even while I claimed to be seeking it. I simply did not see that my intellectual problems were really moral problems in disguise.

19

When the Body Rules the Mind:
The Pursuit of Marriage

It was Alipius who raised the greatest objections to the idea of my getting married. I had lived with a woman for several years, and felt it would be more in keeping with my status as a seeker after truth if I moved away from immorality into marriage—not with her, you understand, but with someone more socially suitable. His argument was that he had tried sex in the past and had not found it very rewarding, and that in any case a wife would be a severe hindrance in our search for truth. He lived, it must be said, an extremely chaste life.

However, I argued against this that many of the wisest men were married. It did not seem to hinder them from seeking the truth, or cut them off from God. Not only that, I pointed out, but the real pleasure of sex was not to be experienced in furtive, snatched encounters, such as he had known, but was greatly enhanced when it involved a lasting relationship (such as I had) and would presumably be even more so if given the honorable status of marriage (such as I intended to have). In the face of those arguments, even Alipius began to weaken.

So the business of finding a wife for me began, fully aided and abetted by my mother. She was anxious to draw me away from the life of immorality which she considered I was now in, and she also hoped that when I got married, I might also be baptized.

But one thing was strange about her attitude to the matter. She used to pray to God to confirm to her in a vision his will about this and that (and often she did receive confirmation in one way or another). Yet where my marriage was concerned, although she prayed about it day and night, no such clear vision from the Lord was given her. She managed a few empty and self-induced fantasies concerning my future wife, but she herself knew these were not divine visions.

Still, the matter went forward. A young woman was asked for, and promised. She was suitable in every way, and I liked her well enough, but she was two years short of marriageable age. I had no choice but to wait.

In fact, of course, I did nothing of the kind. My circle of friends had devised an elaborate plan to live together in a kind of community, to further our search for truth together. But the question of wives—some had wives, and I of course intended to be married, broke up the brotherhood, and the scheme collapsed.

While that was happening, I was going through another very painful experience. If I was to marry a respectable young woman I must, of course, be rid of my lover. When I explained this to her, she took it very badly. She could not believe that I, too, was heartbroken to see her go. She felt I had treated her cruelly (as of course I had) and vowed she would have nothing to do with men ever again. She went home to Africa, leaving our son, a young boy, with me in Milan.

I, too, felt I had been hurt deeply, but my reaction was the opposite of hers. Seeing it would be two years before I could be married, and unable to contemplate such a period of abstinence, I found another lover. It was, like all my attempts at that time to find satisfaction apart from God, an unhappy experience. The pain of separation from my former mistress, whom I still loved, grew stronger rather than weaker. It was a dogged, numbing pain within me, completely spoiling all my attempts at replacing it with a new relationship.

20

The Problem of Evil

At about that time I went through a long period of darkness as I grappled with the problem of the origin of evil. I did not understand that the key to it all was the freedom of the human will. I knew, and clung to the belief, that God was not subject to change or corruption, and that he could not and would not have created anything evil.

So, I wondered, what *was* the origin of evil? If the devil created it, then who but God himself could have created the devil? And if I myself am created by God (who is Goodness itself), how can it be that I so often wish to do evil? Who grafted this evil element into my life? Surely not God. And in any case, could not God, in his omnipotent power, change and convert all the evil in me and everyone else to good? How can evil exist in God's world and against God's will?

Questions like those wracked my brain. I lacked the vital clue that God made us perfect, but gave us freedom of the will; and that we have introduced the principle of evil into our lives by exercising that dangerous gift. Although I could not fully see this, I was more and more convinced of two things: first, that the Manichees were wrong; and second, that when I did find the answer it would lie in the Holy Scriptures and would in some way center on Jesus Christ, God's only Son, and our Lord.

On that basis, it became clear to me that all God has made is good, even corruptible things, like human nature. Because if they were not good to start with, they could not be corrupted: you cannot corrupt something that is already evil. So I could see a distinction. If created beings were the supreme good, like God, they would be incorruptible, as he is. On the other hand, if they were not good at all, there would be nothing in them to be corrupted. They, too, would be incorruptible.

But human beings fall between those two: We are plainly corruptible. So I now saw that as a powerful argument that we were originally made *good*, as the Bible teaches. We are not the supreme good: That is God. But neither are we irreversibly evil: That would put us beyond corruption. But there we are, in the middle, caught in our moral dilemma but unable to save ourselves from it. We are moral beings, made good, in the image of God; but we are corruptible, as we abuse the gift of free will, and are consequently and inevitably corrupted.

More and more, and day by day, I became aware of my nature, because now the Lord was helping me to see it. He began to shine the light of his truth into my life, a light different from anything I had ever known on earth. It was not so much above my understanding intellectually as spiritually.

It was above me because it made me, and I was beneath it because I was made by it. Those who know truth know that light; and those who know that light know the meaning of eternity. *Love* knows it.

21

Light Begins to Dawn

I had sought the truth in philosophy and among the intellectuals of the day. I had dabbled with astrology and become a disciple of the Manichees. But at last I began to stop looking at man and began to look at God—and I became aware that he was helping me to do it, even though I was not yet fit even to begin to come near him.

It was then that the Lord began to "speak" to me, through profound inner convictions.

For instance, on one occasion I became so afraid of the glory and holiness of God that I began to tremble with a mixture of delight and apprehension. It was as though a voice from above said to me, "I am food for the strong. Grow quickly, and you will feed on me. But unlike ordinary food, I shall not become part of you. You will become part of me."

That helped, because I was still bothered by the idea of God being or becoming physical. To me, he was pure Spirit or nothing. So one day I was thinking about this and asking myself, "Is truth actually nonexistent, seeing it is not part either of finite or infinite space?" And again the Lord spoke to me, as though from a vast distance, "Yes, there *is* truth: *I am who I am.*" I heard that, not with my ears, but, as they say, in the heart. It convinced me, so that I could never again doubt it, that truth exists and can be clearly seen and understood through what God has made, including human beings.

That experience led me to reflect on all the created things under God. I saw that none of them had any absolute being (because all were subject to time, decay, death, or destruction), but also that none of them had absolutely no being at all. They existed, but not, as it were, in their own right. All of them depended on God. They exist *only* because he exists. But their existence is not absolute, because they are not what God alone is—eternal. So every creature has a being because he is made by God, but no creature has an absolute being, because he is not what God is.

From such an awareness I drew a clear conclusion. It would be wise for me to hold fast to God, because apart from him I too have no absolute being. But in him I can be what he is, as indeed he had "told" me earlier.

Then came another insight, based on a common experience in daily life, but very revealing to me at that moment. The same bread that is pleasant and refreshing to a healthy man can be nauseating to a man who is sick; the sunlight, which is glorious to the person with sound eyes, is intensely painful to sore or tender eyes. So I realized that God's justice, which is pleasant and refreshing to those who love his ways, may well be offensive

and evil to those who reject him. That understanding seemed to shed light on my continuing struggle with the problem of evil. Surely it could have
its origin not in any thing of substance, but in a
perversion of swerving away from God, a sort of
deflection of the will toward lower things, so that
the goodness of God finally seems evil, and evil,
good.

The trouble was that those thoughts, which I
truly believe came from God, drew me toward
him, but my body and its desires instantly pulled
me away again. I never doubted now that the Lord
himself was the one to whom I ought to commit
myself, but I simply could not do it. My mind
raised endless questions, and those questions God
in his mercy patiently answered. But my body
raised questions too, and it seemed to me at that
time to be stronger than the spirit. After all, it is
through the body and its senses that we perceive
things at all. The problem for me was that those
very senses were distorting my perception of the
truth.

So I took another approach. I felt that my reasoning faculties were being corrupted by my bodily
senses—for instance, whole processions of sensu-
ous images could march across my mind whenever
it tried to raise itself up to spiritual and divine
things.

Yet my mind knew, and cried out, that it preferred the unchangeable to the changeable. For a
moment on one occasion it raised itself above my

habitual sensuality, opening itself to the light. In a blinding flash of insight, at once marvelous and terrifying, my mind saw *"that which is"*: the great inner reality of existence. The "invisible things of God, which are understood by the things that are made." The "substance of things hoped for, the evidence for things not seen."

But I could not hold my eyes on the sight. In a moment or two I was simply looking again at the familiar objects around me. My wonderful experience was only a precious memory, the distant savor of a meal I had seen from afar but had not been able to eat.

22

Misconceptions about Jesus

My view of Jesus was of a man of perfect wisdom far above all other men, but himself not more than a man. I gave him supreme authority as a master, and was greatly impressed by the idea of his virgin birth, which intrigued me by its example of the priority of spiritual over physical things. But I could not see what naturally follows from this, that "the Word was made flesh."

As I saw it, Jesus' life was one in which the Word of God was perfectly present, his soul and mind working in perfect harmony. All that I read about him in the Scripture—his rejoicing and sadness, his deeds and preaching—led me to acknowledge that Christ was a complete and perfect man. I could not yet conceive that he was the truth of God *in person*, but I did believe that above all others he *conveyed* the truth of God.

My friend Alipius, on the other hand, had the opposite difficulty. He thought that Christians believed that, in the incarnation, God became human in such a way that there was neither the soul nor the mind of man in Jesus. All there was was God . . . and flesh. The difficulty such a belief raised for Alipius is obvious. How could Jesus perform the things we read in the Gospels unless he were a living, thinking human being, a man with soul and mind?

So, because he thought that Christians denied it, Alipius moved more slowly and reluctantly than I did toward the faith. Later, of course, both of us realized how wrongly we had grasped the truth about Christ. Surprisingly, perhaps, Alipius realized that fact before I did. It was a long while before I came to understand what the true Christian teaching was about "the Word made flesh."

My basic trouble was an obsession with being intellectual, or appearing to be so, puffed up with my own cleverness. I expected God to reward my "wisdom." But where was my humility? Where was my love of God, who owed me nothing? I seemed to be two people, one wanting to be right with God, the other just wanting to be right.

It was then that the apostle Paul came to my aid. I had determined to read again all his books, and I found they spoke with amazing relevance to my position. Here, in the letter to the Romans, for instance, Paul faced questions that the Platonists and other philosophers never even asked. But they were questions that tormented me. When I read those verses, they seemed to echo my own despairing cries: "My mind delights in the law of God, but I see another law at work in my body, which rejects it, and leads me captive to the law of sin which resides in my body. Who shall deliver me from this body of death?" And then came the answer. "I thank God, through Christ Jesus our Lord."

The books of the philosophers never speak of such inner conflicts. They do not tell of troubled spirits, of "a broken and contrite heart." No one lifts his voice in their pages to sing out, "Shall not my soul wait on God, for from him comes my salvation . . . He is my God and my Savior, my Protector. I shall never more be moved." In their books you will not hear a voice saying, "Come to me, all you who labor and are weary"—because they despise anyone who is, as Jesus claimed to be, "meek and humble of heart." Why are such things not found in their writings? Because God "has hidden them from the wise and learned, and revealed them to babes."

As I read Paul's words, and the other words of

Scripture, I realized in a clearer way my position. It was one thing to sit, as I had done, on some wooded mountaintop and view the land of peace far away, without knowing the way there or being able to overcome the impenetrable barrier raised by error and sin. It was quite another thing, and infinitely better, to leave that apparently secure mountaintop and, trusting God to lead the way, walk securely toward the land of peace. At last, at last, I felt I was on the journey.

CHAPTER FIVE

The Moment
of Truth

Augustine's conversion occurred when he was thirty-two, so the process that led to it was a long one. His account of the days leading up to it, and the actual event itself, is one of the great spiritual testimonies of Christian history. From his prayer that God would "make him holy . . . but not yet," to the moment when some children chanting a playground rhyme drove him to open his copy of the letters of Paul, his story has all the qualities of a devotional classic. Yet all is told with disarming modesty. Augustine makes no attempt to gild the lily.

A number of distinguished names play a role in the story. Ambrose was one of them, the bishop of Milan whose hymns are still sung today. Another was Simplicianus, who prepared Augustine for baptism. He was for many years Ambrose's assistant, and after the great man's death, when Simplicianus himself was an old man, he succeeded Ambrose as bishop of Milan.

But a decisive influence was that of a layman, a new convert. Marius Victorinus was a noted intellectual of the time, a distinguished Neo-Platonist and rhetorician. His conversion to Christianity, and especially his public confession of it, caused a great stir in Milan and evidently contributed to the repentance of the still-wavering Augustine.

23

The Last Steps:
The Power of Testimony

I had reached the point of no return. The word of the Lord penetrated to the root of my being. I felt that God was boring in on me on every side, giving me no way of escape. I no longer had doubts about the eternal life of God, nor about the relationship of physical substance to a spiritual being. In my head I was converted. I could find no argument against the truth. Yet where my earthly life was concerned, everything remained unresolved. My heart was still contaminated with the subtle influences of the world and the flesh. Try as I would, I could not imagine life without sexual gratification. I could find no fault in the One who is the Way, the Savior of the world, but I could not bring myself to follow him through the narrow gate that leads to life.

At that point God directed me toward an old and wise man, Simplicianus, a person who from his youth had led a devout Christian life. It was he who had led Bishop Ambrose to the Lord many years before. Now, in his old age, he seemed to me to have the long experience and spiritual discernment that could guide me through my present confusion.

So I went to him, and explained my dilemma: how I had come through many experiences and setbacks to this situation, that I no longer found any satisfaction or pleasure in worldly success or acclaim, that I was disgusted with my own way of life and especially that my body so often ruled my will, that nothing any longer gave me the joy that the Lord did. But, I added, I was trapped by sexual lust, and, being morally weak, constantly chose the soft and easier option.

In short, I said, I knew now that I had found the "pearl of great price" of which Jesus spoke, but I doubted whether I was prepared to pay the price of acquiring it.

Simplicianus listened and then, instead of answering my questions, picked up a passing reference I had made to the works of a famous master of rhetoric in Rome, Victorinus, whom I believed had died a Christian.

Simplicianus saw at once that my problem was my unwillingness to humble myself, or to believe that the truth is hidden from human wisdom but revealed to babes. For that reason he began to tell me the story of how Victorinus came to Christ.

Victorinus was one of the most outstanding scholars of the time, distinguished in the liberal sciences, a respected student and critic of the great philosophers, a tutor to many of the most noble senators. For all those services in high office he was marked out for an unusual honor: his statue was erected in the Forum in Rome.

All his life he had been a worshiper of idols and a devout follower of the pagan religion, as, in fact, were almost all the leading figures in Rome at that time. Indeed, he championed the cause of the old religions with thunderous eloquence.

Later, in his old age, Victorinus began to study the Holy Scriptures and to seek out and pore over other Christian writings. He found them enormously attractive and convincing, so much so that he came to Simplicianus privately and said, "I would like you to know that I have become a Christian." Simplicianus, however, was not readily convinced of that.

"I will never believe it, nor accept you as a Christian, until I see you publicly in the church of Christ," he said.

Victorinus laughed. "So it's the walls of the church, then, that makes people into Christians?"

But Simplicianus stood his ground for many weeks, the elderly intellectual claiming that he was indeed a Christian, and the Christian minister saying that he was not a Christian until he was prepared to join the visible Body of Christ. Often Victorinus would end the argument with his remark about the church's walls. The truth was, as he well knew, that he was afraid to offend his friends, the followers of the pagan gods, who might turn against him if he renounced their religion and acknowledged Christ publicly.

Eventually Victorinus came across the warning of Christ in the Gospels, that he would not confess before his holy angels those who were afraid to confess him before men. The old man began to fear that he might in the end be denied because of his unwillingness to confess Christ publicly. He also saw that it would be a grievous thing formerly to have joined in the sacrilegious rites of the pagan temple freely and proudly, but now to have refused to receive the sacraments of the church humbly, as bearers of the Word.

So he surprised Simplicianus one day by saying, "Come on, let's go to church. I am resolved to be a Christian." Delighted, Simplicianus went with him to the church, where he was enrolled for instruction in the faith. Soon he turned in his name as a candidate for baptism, intending to demonstrate his new birth—both to the amazement of the people of Rome and to the joy of the Christians.

When the day came for his profession of faith in baptism, the priests made an offer to Victorinus of a more private ceremony to spare him too much public attention (a concession that occasionally was offered in suitable circumstances). But he refused, saying he would rather profess his faith in the presence of the whole assembly. After all, he said, what he had taught in the past was public knowledge. Why should this much greater matter of salvation not be confessed publicly?

When he rose up to make his profession (which at Rome was done in a set form of memorized words), the whole congregation recognized him. "It's Victorinus!" they whispered to each other across the church. For a moment they could not contain their surprise and pleasure, but shouted out for joy. But as he began to speak, the congregation hushed, not wanting to miss a single word. He declared his faith before them with great confidence, and instantly the whole congregation took him to their hearts.

24

A Chain of Iron

The story Simplicianus told me had exactly the effect he had hoped for. I was suddenly burning with desire to follow the example of Victorinus. Later, during the time of the Emperor Julian, Simplicianus told me Victorinus had to choose whether to continue to teach rhetoric or to concentrate on the Scriptures, since an imperial edict now forbade Christians to teach literature or rhetoric. Of course Victorinus chose the way of God's Word. I counted him blessed, rather than resolute, to be able so easily and clearly to settle the issue.

I longed that I might be given a similarly clear choice. I felt myself bound by a chain of iron, a chain forged by the Enemy out of my own unruly will. What happens to us is that impure desires spring from our misdirected affections, and by giving in to them we create a habit, which in turn becomes a kind of necessity. That process bound me like the links of a chain. My new-found will, which longed to serve God, was not yet strong enough to overcome my old corrupted will, hard tempered by long practice. So my two wills struggled—the new against the old, the spiritual against the carnal—and in the process nearly tore my spirit apart.

That was just what the apostle Paul had said. "The flesh lusts against the Spirit, and the Spirit against the flesh." I was experiencing what he and others had experienced before. I was not unique.

The trouble was quite simply a failure of my will. I was like a sleeper who wakes and fully intends to get up and get on with the day's activities, but in fact turns over for another nap. My mind was convinced, but my body would not follow its signals. On every side the Lord showed me what I should do, and all I could say in response was "Yes, yes, I agree. Soon. I shall do it very soon. Have patience with me just a little while longer." But in fact the *soon* grew longer and longer and the *little while* stretched out into a long while.

I found that the law of habit is a vicious one, a kind of "law of sin," which can hold the mind of human beings even against their will. We pay a heavy price for having first slipped into sin so willingly. As my favorite apostle put it, "Wretched man that I am, who shall deliver me from this body of death?" I knew, as he knew, that the only answer was the grace of the Lord Jesus Christ.

"Make Me Holy . . . But Not Yet"

The story of Victorinus had a great effect on me, but it was reinforced by an experience a few days later. Alipius and I were visited by a friend from Africa, Pontitianus. He had a high position in the emperor's household. I cannot remember what the occasion of his visit was, but I can vividly recall his picking up my book of Paul's epistles, which I had by me on the table. He seemed pleased to see it there and a bit surprised. When I explained I was giving a great deal of time to the reading of Scripture, he took the opportunity to explain that he was a Christian and recently had the opportunity to study the works of an Egyptian monk, Antony. Neither Alipius nor I had ever heard of him nor of the great spiritual revival that had followed his ministry. Thousands of men had entered the monasteries to give their lives to prayer and service, even in the heart of the desert.

More than that, Pontitianus told us, there was a flourishing monastery here in Milan, just outside the city walls, under the pastoral care of Ambrose. We, who lived in Milan, knew nothing of it.

He then went on to tell how he had been on a visit to Treves, with three other agents in public affairs, while the emperor was at the afternoon games in the circus. The four had split into two's and were walking casually near the town when the other two men came upon a poor cottage, where several devout Christians lived in complete self-denial. They were "the poor in spirit," who shall "inherit the kingdom of heaven."

There they were shown a book of the life of Antony, which one of the companions of Pontitianus began to read. Doing so, he was overcome with determination to lead a similarly dedicated life, not "one day," or "soon," or "in a little while," but there and then. He explained his intention to his friend, saying he had decided to break with his present life and ambitions and join this little community immediately—without even returning to town. His friend, to his surprise, said he would join him.

When Pontitianus and his companion caught up with them, they tried to persuade them to return to the emperor's court. But when they saw how sincerely convinced the two of them were they tearfully congratulated them, promised to support them with their prayers, and rather reluctantly made their way back to the palace.

The first two, filled with a new vision, remained in the poor cottage. Both of them, as it happened, were engaged to be married, but when their fiancées heard what had happened, they also decided to give their lives to God's service and entered a community.

Just hearing that story was a hideous rebuke to

me. It forced me to look at myself and to hate what I saw. For so many years, ever since I was nineteen, I had claimed to be searching for the truth. Yet here I was, still delaying, still putting it off, while these men had responded to God's call instantly—not over years or months or even weeks, but within *minutes.* From my teens I had prayed to God for purity, it is true. But I had always added a qualifier. "Lord," I would pray, "make me content, but not yet." I was afraid that God would instantly answer and instantly deliver me. What I really wanted was not that my lust should be quenched so much as glutted.

I had fooled myself that I put off making a decision because I was not sure which was the right way to go. Yet here I was, absolutely sure of the way, convinced of the truth, and yet still prevaricating, still praying, "Lord make me holy . . . but not yet."

26

One Day in the Garden

There was a garden to our lodging, which we had free use of since the owner of the house lived elsewhere. One day, during this period of my spiritual turmoil, I made my way into the garden accompanied by Alipius. I felt I had arrived at a crisis. My voice was strained and strange, my face flushed, and tears were beginning to wet my cheeks.

"Look," I said to Alipius, "look at the state we are in. The uneducated and simple are committed Christians, and we, with all our learning, are still trapped by flesh and blood."

We sat as far from the house as possible, I groaning and weeping, he surprised and anxious. I now could see that everything came down to a problem of the will. We can do nothing unless we will it, from raising a hand to setting out on a journey over land and sea. We must have the will to do it, a determined and strong will, not a half-hearted, ambiguous, indecisive one.

Where our bodies are concerned, unless there is some physical weakness or deformity, the will and the power to do something are virtually one and the same. I think of lifting my hand, and I do it.

Why, then, I wondered, was it that the mind itself was so slow to obey the will. Could it be because when we will a simple physical movement we will it *entirely*, the means and the end, whereas when we will a spiritual or moral issue, we may will it only in part, or half-heartedly? It is then the indecisiveness that thwarts the action? We do not do it because deep down we are not sure we want to do it.

So I sat there in the garden, in a private world of my own. My old nature, the body of death which I had inherited as an heir of Adam and his sin, struggled to retain a hold on me, while the Lord redoubled his inner call to me to have done with this old nature and rise to a new one. I kept saying to myself, "Come on, let it happen now, let it happen *now*," and as I spoke I almost resolved to do it. But I did not. Yet I did not slide back into my old nature either. It was as though I stood outside myself and watched the struggle. I was hanging there suspended between dying to death and living to life. I was surprised how powerful was the restraint of my old evil habits and how subtly they tugged at me, holding me back.

"Just think," they whispered, "if you take this step, you will never again experience the pleasures of sexual indulgence. From that moment, all those things will be forbidden you forever. Can you really live without us?" And although I knew they were merely toys and frivolities, compared to eternal values, their voices were insistent and their appeal held me back.

But it was a dwindling power; nothing like it had been on previous occasions. It was as though I could see in front of me a better vision, a picture of a whole new kind of life, a life of purity and self-discipline. Nor was it a gloomy or negative scene. Far from it. It was actually enticing, but not in a dissolute way. I could see, in the vision, scores of people of all ages, young men and women, elderly widows, older men, but all of them smiling and welcoming, apparently overflowing with inner joy.

A voice said to me, "Can't you do what all of

these people have done? And yet, *they* have not done it, certainly not in their own strength. They have come to this joy through a strength given to them by the Lord their God.

"Your trouble is that you are trying to achieve such a state in your own strength, and consequently you are achieving nothing at all. Cast yourself on God alone and trust him. He will not hold back and let you fall. But you have to trust him completely. Then, and only then, will he receive and heal you."

I hesitated, hearing again those malicious whispers in my ear. "Can you really live without us forever?"

But the heavenly voice spoke again. "Close your ears to those murmurs. They come from your fallen, sinful nature. Put it to death. I know they speak to all kinds of sinful delights, but they are contrary to the law of the Lord your God."

That strange debate went on within me, while poor Alipius sat at my side waiting silently for the battle to be resolved.

At that point I needed to be alone, and I said something to that effect (I can't remember the words) and left Alipius, so that there was no human restraint on me at all. I flung myself to the ground under a fig tree and wept bitterly, a "sacrifice acceptable to You, O Lord." I cried out loud, in some such words as these: "How long, Lord? How long? Will You be angry with me forever? Do not remember my former sins."

It was indeed those former sins and their present power that seemed to be holding me back. So I went on praying. "How long, Lord? Tomorrow and tomorrow? Why not now? Why not at this moment make an end of my uncleanness?"

Then, as I prayed, I heard a voice, like a little boy or girl in a nearby house, repeating some words by heart in a singsong manner: "Take it up and read it. Take it up and read it."

I was arrested by the sound. I had never heard those words used in a children's game. My bitterness and tears stopped. I got up, convinced that the message was from heaven and that it was telling me to read from the first chapter I should find on opening my book of Paul's writings. I remembered how Antony had been told—in a rather similar way, by a passage in the Gospels that was apparently meant for him at one point in his life—"Go, sell all you have, and give to the poor, and you shall have treasure in heaven. And come, and follow me."

So I went back to the table where Alipius was sitting and picked up the book of Paul's writings which I had left there. I took it quickly in my hand, opened it, and read silently from the chapter that my eyes first lighted on. "Not in orgies and drunkenness, not in promiscuity and lust, not in anger and jealousy: but put on the Lord Jesus Christ, and make no provision for the flesh and its desires."

I needed to read no further. Instantly, as I

reached the end of the sentence, all the darkness of my former doubts was dispelled, as if a clear and insistent light had flooded my heart. I must turn from the old; I must put on the new; and I must do it now.

I shut the book, though marking the page, and told Alipius in a quiet and calm voice exactly what had happened. In his turn, he told me what had been going on in his own heart, which I knew nothing about. He then asked if he could see the passage I had read—but he read on a little further to some words I had not known were there. "Now him who is weak in the faith take with you." He applied this to himself, he told me, and at once, without any hesitation, he joined me in my new-found purpose and commitment.

Immediately we went into the house to find my mother and tell her what had happened. Needless to say, she was overjoyed. As she said, the Lord is "able to do more abundantly than we either ask or think." She said that because she had limited her prayers to my conversion. But so deeply had God worked in me that I had instantly forsaken all human ambitions, even the desire for a wife, and had decided to dedicate myself to that very rule of life which the Lord had shown my mother many years before that I should accept, an acceptance which even she had scarcely the faith to believe would ever actually happen.

CHAPTER SIX

Believing . . .
and Grieving

Augustine's conversion brought him great joy and a sense of relief, but it seems safe to say that it gave equal joy to his mother. His baptism, together with his best friend Alipius, and his son Adeodatus, was an occasion of celebration. Sadly for Augustine, that event was quite soon followed by his mother's death, which proved a severe test of his newfound faith.

The *Confessions* end there. The prodigal has come home. The one who had watched over and prayed for him all his life had gone to her rest contented.

Of course there is much more to the life of Augustine. He founded a monastic order, still with us today. He was ordained presbyter in A.D. 391 by Bishop Valerius of Hippo. Then, when the bishop died four years later, Augustine was appointed in his place. He exercised an enormous influence on the church of his day, training clergy (twelve of his men became bishops in Africa) and writing a formidable number of books to refute heresies and argue the case for apostolic Christianity.

27

The Effect on our Friends

The first decision I made after my conversion was to forsake as quickly as possible the profession and teaching of rhetoric. I saw now that it was little more than a matter of marketing a lying tongue: using the gift of eloquence not to serve law and peace, but to win legal battles. My conversion happened about three weeks before the end of the school term, and although it was painful to do so, I felt in fairness to my pupils I ought to complete the term's work.

I say *painful*, and it was that in two senses. Spiritually, because all desire for money-making

had gone from me, and that was really the main
motive in the whole business. But also physically,
because I had some trouble with my lungs, which
made breathing almost impossible. That circum-
stance, however, gave me a completely valid ex-
cuse to limit my teaching and other work, and
thus made the whole process easier. It also helped
me avoid the apparent ostentation of announcing
that, having become a Christian, I was abandoning
my highly paid and prestigious post.

My mind was set free from the biting cares of
ambition and wealth, and also from the temptations of impurity and lust. I simply sat in my room
and prattled away to the Lord like a talkative child.

Our two friends and companions, Verecundus
and Nebridius, and not, of course, shared our
experiences in the garden. Verecundus was the
more upset, because he saw that it would end our
association. He was drawn toward the faith, but
although his wife was a Christian, he saw her as
the main stumbling-block in the way of his conversion. That was because, as he put it, "I don't want
to be less of a Christian than you two, and that I
can't be as a married man."

We tried to reassure him, telling him he could
be totally faithful to Christ in his present married
state. But at that time he could not be persuaded.

He was kind enough to lend us his country
house, at Cassiciacum, however, and there we
were able to live while we worked out the implications of our conversion. Later on, in our absence,

he became ill, but in that sickness, which proved fatal, he became a true Christian. We took this in one way as a sign of God's mercy to him and to us. Certainly we should have been distraught, had he, who had been so close to us, died outside the faith.

Nebridius also came to Christ. He had been caught up in that detestable heresy which believed that Jesus did not truly take human flesh, but was only a spiritual being on earth. But at the time of our conversion he was fighting free of that delusion and was genuinely seeking the truth. Soon after, he too was converted and subsequently led all his household in Africa to Christ. But then, like Verecundus, he was taken ill and died, and lives now in paradise.

I remember him with love, and delight to think that he is indeed living with the Lord as a true son in the heaven he often used to ask me about— me, who was then as ignorant as he was of spiritual things. Now he has no need to bring his questions to so inept and inexpert a guide, but can drink wisdom to the full from the wellspring of all knowledge. And I dare hope that he also remembers me.

28

The Joy of the Spirit

When the school term ended, I was able to dedicate myself to filling my heart, too, with spiritual riches. I wrote many letters, some of them to dear Nebridius, trying to explain what God had shown us and bearing testimony to his grace in our lives. And the Lord worked on me, on all my roughness and pride, subduing and humbling me, sometimes with sharp goads, sometimes with blessings that made me rejoice.

I rediscovered the Psalms of David, those wonderful hymns of faith, whose words rebuke our pride. Those are the books I associate most with our stay in Cassiciacum. I turned David's prayers into my own, reciting them aloud, as though in hope that all humanity would respond to their message.

Of course, I was as yet a novice in God's love, a newly arrived foreigner in the state of grace, as was Alipius. But my mother remained with us, a woman of mature faith, with the patience that comes with age, the gentle understanding of a mother, and the devotion of a true Christian. As we pursued our catechetical studies, slowly being instructed in the faith, she was our constant support and encourager.

I also found myself being opened up to the Holy Spirit. It was true I had received salvation. God had sent his Son to die for sin, raised him from the dead, and exalted him to glory . . . from whence, the Scripture says, "he would pour upon us the Comforter, the Spirit of truth." That had happened, the Spirit had been given, but I was not aware of him. I was forgiven, but I did not yet have perfect peace, partly because I was anxious about those I had in the past led into sin and partly for the recollection of my own past sin.

But there, in the country house of Verecundus, the Holy Spirit began to do his sweet work and to bring joy to my heart. Yet it was through pain that I came closest to him.

It came on me suddenly, a most terrible toothache, such as I had never experienced before. It was so acute that it made me speechless. At that time, tortured with the pain, it came to me to call on all my Christian friends to pray for my healing to the God of all health. I wrote my request on wax letters, which I gave to them so that they could join me in prayer. And the moment we bowed our knees to pray—yes, immediately—the pain simply disappeared. I was awestruck. What kind of pain had that been? Where had it come from? By what power had it been taken away instantly?

But deep within me it spoke the reassurance I needed. God's will was being done in me. My heart lifted up to him in praise and joy, rooted in faith.

29

God's Mercy in Baptism

At the end of the grape harvest, when the new term was due to begin in Milan, I wrote to let my students' parents know that I would not be returning to teaching. I also wrote to Bishop Ambrose, telling him of my former errors and present commitment, and asking him which books he would recommend that I read in order to grow in grace. He suggested the prophet Isaiah, I imagine because he speaks most clearly of the coming gospel and God's purpose for the Gentiles. However, when I started the book I found it difficult and obscure, and put it aside, intending to tackle it later when I was better instructed in the Word of God.

The time had now come for my name to be handed in for baptism, so we left the country and made our way back to Milan. Two others were to be baptized with me, to my great joy in both cases.

The first was, of course, Alipius, who was now a marvelous, humble, and believing Christian. The second was my own son, Adeodatus—and what a miracle of God's generosity that was. He was now fifteen, the child of my immoral association, but a young man of great gifts, intelligence, and spiritual maturity. That was little thanks to me, I am afraid, for all I gave him was the sin out of which he was begotten. That he was brought up in the fear of the Lord was entirely of God's grace, who led us both to it even when we were ourselves blind to the truth.

It was a great joy, soon after his baptism, to write a book with him, a kind of dialogue between us called "About the Master." God knows that every word in that book which is put into my son's mouth he did in fact speak, showing at only sixteen an almost miraculous insight into truth. He died as a young man, in earthly terms unfulfilled; but I have great confidence that he is now fulfilled in heaven.

At our baptism the three of us stood together, because in the realm of grace we were all the same age, newborn babies. Immediately all anxiety about my former life and its sins was taken away, and in the following days I experienced an indescribable joy as I went more deeply into God's marvelous plan of salvation.

30

An Occasion for Celebration

Often when hymns and psalms were being sung in church I would break into tears of joy, both at

the sweetness of the singing and also at the marvelous truths contained in the words.

The church in Milan, which we joined, was in
any case in a mood of celebration and praise. About
a year before, Justina, mother of the young emperor Valentinian, had taken up the Arian heresy
and set out to try to remove Bishop Ambrose,
who, of course, entirely rejected the false Arian
teachings about the nature of Christ. The congregation would take turns guarding the church and
its precincts, fearing that her servants would try
do harm to the bishop or arrest him. My mother,
with others, prayed literally day and night that
the enemy would be restrained.

Actually it was during that time that the church
in Milan first began to use hymns and psalms in
its services, which up to then had been done only
in the eastern church. They were brought in to
provide some relief during the lengthy vigils of
prayer, but were retained afterward, and eventually the practice was taken up by almost every
congregation throughout the rest of the world.

The church was delivered from that time of
anxiety in a most remarkable way. The Lord
showed Ambrose in a vision the place where the
bodies of two martyrs, Gervasius and Protasius,
had been hidden many years before. When the
secret tomb was found and opened, it became
clear that God had preserved the two bodies from
corruption. Ambrose arranged for them to be
moved and buried with due honor in the church.

It was while the procession was on its way that a remarkable miracle occurred. A blind man, someone very well known in the city, a man who had been blind many years, asked his guide to lead him to the procession and then got permission to touch the coffin of the martyrs with his handkerchief. When he had done that, and put the handkerchief to his eyes, he shouted out that he could see—a fact soon evident to the entire crowd.

The result was that the whole city was moved to amazement, and Justina herself, although not going so far as to abandon her heresy completely and join herself to the church, nevertheless did abandon her persecution of the bishop.

I suppose it was the memory of events like those, which happened before my conversion, but about which I had known—without recognizing them as signs and confirmations of the faith—that made me weep during the singing of the hymns. It was partly regret, but mostly joy that now at last I was breathing in Your grace and love, O Lord, insofar as one can breathe it purely in this house of clay.

31

The Death of My Mother

We were joined in our small household by a young man from my home town, Euodius, who had been converted and baptized just before us. He, too, intended to follow a rule of life, and together we determined to go back to Carthage and try to find ways of serving the Lord there.

We began with the long overland journey, finally arriving at Ostia, at the mouth of the Tiber River, where we decided to spend a little while preparing ourselves for the sea trip.

One day in the house at Ostia my mother and I were standing in a window looking over the garden. As sometimes happens, we embarked on a profound conversation. Its topic was eternal life, the life of the saints in heaven.

As we spoke, our conversation soared to remarkable heights, even, in a kind of irresistible progress, above the usual limitations of the human mind. We talked on, admiring the wonder of God's acts, and then turned inward, probing into our own souls to see there, too, the hand of God at work. We became aware, intensely aware, of the *present:* not what has been in the past, nor what shall be hereafter, but what *is,* as God himself is.

For a time our conversation left human language

behind. I truly believe we tasted, in some small way, eternity itself. Then we sighed and returned to the sound of everyday words, with all the limitations they necessarily have. But in those words we tried to recapture our experience. It seemed to us that eternity is the state where all the tumult of the world is silent, every human tongue still, every human thought set aside or bypassed, all dreams and imaginations and signs and symbols discarded—and in that magnificent silence *God alone speaks*—not through human agents, written words, voice of angel or parable, but rather God himself is making all things known.

Beside that eternal reality, all the joys of earth, even the purest and holiest ones, fade into insignificance. Such an experience gives to his people for the rest of eternity the ecstasy that had been ours for a brief moment of understanding. Does not this fulfill the invitation, "Enter into the joy of the Lord"? But can such a thing happen while we still reside in mortal flesh? Surely it must await that time when we shall rise, changed, "in the twinkling of an eye," into the life of the resurrection.

So we spoke, perhaps not precisely in those words. But God knows that we entered that day into a shared experience which made this life itself seem inferior, and which we described in words like those.

When the moment was over, my mother spoke.

"Augustine, my son, as far as I am concerned,

I no longer find any delight in this life.
don't know what there is left for me to do
nor even why God keeps me here, now that all
my earthly hopes are fulfilled. The only thing that
made me want to go on living a little while longer
was the hope of seeing you become a true Christian before I died. Now God has not only granted
that, but more—because I see you turning aside
from earthly ambitions and giving yourself wholly
to his service. So why should I go on living?"

I cannot remember how I replied, but within
five days or so she became ill with a fever. It was
so serious that for a while she lapsed into uncon-
sciousness, and we all ran to her bedside. Soon
she revived, and seeing myself and my brother
Navigius at her side, she first asked us, "Where
was I?" and then, fixing her eyes on us, said, "You
will bury your mother here."

I was silent, but my brother said something to
the effect that he hoped my mother would have
the happiness of dying and being buried in her
home country. My mother looked at him anxiously
and then said, "Lay this body wherever you wish,
and don't have any anxiety about it. All I ask is
that you remember me in the sacrament, wherever
you are." She then fell silent, being very weak and
increasingly ill.

For me, however, that brief conversation was a
matter for praise. I knew how much, over the
years, my mother had worried about her burial
arrangements. She had obtained and prepared a

place alongside her husband's grave, and had always hoped that, at the end of our distant journeys in Italy, God would grant that her earthly remains should join his in the soil of Tagaste, in North Africa.

I do not know when she abandoned that somewhat superstitious hope, but some time later a friend of hers in Ostia told me that one day they had discussed the matter together. The friend suggested that she must be afraid of dying and being buried so far from her homeland. My mother replied, "Nowhere is far from God. I'm not the least bit worried that he won't know well enough on the day of judgment where to find my body and raise it to new life."

She was ill a little over a week. Then, at the age of fifty-six—when I was thirty-three—God released her holy soul from the prison of her weak and weary body.

32

Grieving and Believing

When my mother died, I bent over her and closed her eyes. At once an indescribable wave of sorrow flooded my heart and overflowed into tears. As her life slipped away, my son Adeodatus, who

was standing by the bed, broke into a loud lamen-
tation, but I and the others quieted him, and soon
he too was composed. I repressed my tears, and
even at the funeral we did not encourage demon-
strations of inconsolable sadness, such as wailing
or screaming with grief. We considered such things
inappropriate for those who do not think of death
as the end of everything and thus a time of abject
loss. After all, my mother had not died unhappily.
In one sense, she had not died at all, because we
all knew that her true faith would bring her to
eternal life.

What hurt me inwardly (more than I was prepared to show) was the sudden breaking-off of
our marvelously close and intimate relationship,
the end of something precious and unique to us.
She had called me her "good son," but how much
better was she a mother to me, and how much I
valued all she had done for me over the years.

After she died, when Adeodatus was calmed,
Euodius began to sing the psalm, "I will sing unto
You, O Lord, of mercy and judgment," and all the
household joined us, including many of the believers, and while others were discussing the
funeral arrangements I spoke a word to those who
had gathered. I think the neighbors were rather
surprised, even concluding that I lacked a proper
sense of grief. But I knew what was in my heart,
even though my face did not betray it.

Indeed, when my mother's body was carried
out, I followed it without tears—not even at the

eucharist near the grave, which was the custom there. But I was desperately sad inwardly, and I begged the Lord to take away my grief, which I felt to be a denial of our faith.

I remember hearing somewhere that the Greeks believed that a bath helped to draw grief from the mind, but it did not help me. However, soon after bathing I fell asleep—and when I woke, the edge had gone from my grief. As I lay in bed, a verse of one of Ambrose's hymns came to my mind and helped to console me:

O Lord who made the earth we love
And set the sun and moon above,
You fill the passing day with light
But shade our eyes to sleep by night;

Sleep which restores our body's powers
For labor in the daylight hours,
And calms our overburdened mind
Of every care which it may find.

I began to remember my mother as she used to be in my childhood: so devout a Christian, so gentle and caring a parent. Then, at last and unbidden, the tears began to come. All the tears I had repressed were suddenly given permission, as it were, to flow. They were wept only for God's ears, and for one hour, but I cannot and do not count them sinful or unfaithful.

Now, looking back, I can still find tears at her

memory, but they are tears of a different kind. Of course I still remember her holy life and strong faith, but I must also recall that she, like every one of us, was a sinner, and that her only hope of heaven was through the forgiveness won for us on the Cross by the Son of God himself, who now sits at the Father's right hand and "ever makes intercession for us."

Her only hope was in that perfect sacrifice, by which "the indictment of our sins is blotted out" and our enemy Satan is trodden under foot, and through which we are "more than conquerors." To the sacrament of our redemption she clung fast all her life by the bonds of faith. May nothing ever stand between her and God's love. Indeed, I believe God has already answered that prayer for her. My mother would not say she had never sinned; but she would and did say that her sins were all forgiven for his sake.

So she rests in peace with her husband Patricius, whom she won for the Lord. These two, my parents in this fleeting life, my brother and sister in the church, my fellow citizens in the new Jerusalem.

PART II

CHAPTER SEVEN

Teacher
and Preacher

This section of the book contains a small selection, a sample, of the vast body of writings on the Christian life, on spirituality, on major questions of the faith, that Augustine left us.

We have already seen how important the Psalms were to him at one stage in his life. That interest is reflected here as well, as are a number of the questions he had wrestled with during the years of his pilgrimage to faith.

What emerges most of all, however, is the heart of the pastor and teacher. Augustine always *applied* the truths of the Bible—not always, one has to admit, according to the best principles of Bible interpretation as we know them today. But he used his biblical understanding to open up issues, to warn, rebuke, encourage, and inspire in a way that few modern preachers and writers can equal. The bishop of Hippo, who died in A.D. 430, speaks to us today.

The Dangers of Gossip

One of the great examples set me by my mother was her concern to use speech and conversation to make peace rather than destroy it.

She won her mother-in-law over by refusing to speak ill of her even when she was being constantly criticized—largely, she later discovered, through malicious rumors circulated by some of the servants. Eventually patience and a gentle tongue won her over.

It was my mother's rule of life to report to other people only what might help reconcile them to their enemies, and never what would serve to stir up strife. If she spoke separately to two people who were in dispute, she would tell the one only the positive and helpful things the other had said. It may seem a tiny virtue. My experience, however, is that most people in such circumstances, perhaps as one of the consequences of fallen human nature, tend to pass on the most inflammatory parts of what they have heard—and even to embellish them.

There is no way to peace, it has been said; rather, peace is the way.

34

It Is Not *What* but
How We Know that Matters

Lord, You are not pleased with someone simply because that person is knowledgeable. In fact, it would be possible for one to know everything there is to know in the whole wide world, except for knowing You, and consequently know nothing. Just as another person could live in blissful ignorance of the great sum of human knowledge, *but know You,* and be both happy and content.

After all, who is better placed—the person who owns a tree and gives You thanks for all the good things it provides; or the one who owns a similar tree and knows its weight and dimensions down to the last leaf, but does not realize that You are its Creator and that it is through You that he or she has the use of it? In essence, the latter person is ignorant, though full of facts, and the former person wise, though a bit short on details.

So in general we can say that the most important knowledge is knowledge of You, O Lord. A person who has that, as Paul said, "possesses nothing yet owns everything." We may not know the course of the Great Bear through the sky, we may not be able to analyze chemical elements nor measure continents, but we can know You, our Creator and God, who plots the courses of the stars, creates the elements, and shapes the land and sky and sea. Better to know the Planner than the Plan.

35

Obeying God and Caesar

There is obviously a difference between the law of man and the law of God. Human law is based on a tremendous variety of customs and practices, whereas God's law is consistent and absolute.

That doesn't mean, of course, that we can disregard human laws, the laws of our state and government, with impunity. A law that is ratified by the constitution of a city or nation is the will of the whole body, and it is unacceptable that individuals should set themselves against the community of which they are only a part.

So Christians respect their nation's laws, but they do not give them precedence over the law of God. When God commands anything, it must be done. Yes, it must be done even if it is against the rules or customs of our society, even if it is completely without precedent. If God commands us to do something that we have stopped doing for one reason or another, then we must take it up again. If God commands something to be set up that doesn't at present exist, then we must set it up.

The reason is simple. It is completely lawful for an earthly ruler to decree something that is totally new, and his subjects are bound to obey it unless it is completely against the common good—and as in general we are agreed that an ordered society depends on our obedience to the law, it is unlikely that an individual could justify opposing it. So if we give that kind of unqualified obedience to law made and enforced by human beings, how much more should we unhesitatingly obey everything that God commands. In the hierarchy of human society the greater power (for instance, the state) receives obedience from the lesser (for instance, the individual). As God's power is infinite, he can claim obedience from every creature—and no argument of personal preference or general good carries any weight at all against that.

36

The Language of the Heart

At school I had to learn Greek, and I hated it. People told me how wonderful the stories of Homer were, but to be honest I didn't enjoy them. I dare say the plots were gripping, the dialogue witty and subtle, but it was all wasted on me. It is hard to enjoy a book when every sentence represents an obstacle course and you are spending more time in the dictionary than you are on the story. And it doesn't help when a teacher is standing over you with a ruler, giving you a smart rap every time you get it wrong.

Of course, there was a time when I had to learn Latin, too. But that was easy. No one stood over me. There was no pressure or compulsion. My nurses spoke it to me as they bathed me or changed my clothes. My parents chattered in it at the dinner table. When I did something clever, it was in words of Latin that they praised me. When someone made me laugh, the joke was in that familiar tongue.

So naturally, as time went on, when I wanted to say something or praise someone or make them laugh, I did it in Latin—probably getting it quite wrong at first, but nobody minded. It was *my* language, the language of the heart, and I learned it from talkers, not teachers. The moral of that seems to be that curiosity, freedom, and enjoyment are better ways of learning than necessity, fear, or compulsion.

Then, I ask myself, is this true in the spiritual realm? Do I learn the ways of God best by fear, duty, and compulsion? Or by freedom and joy, simply being at home in my Father's house? Can I "pick up" the language of the Spirit as I picked up my mother tongue?

I decided that the answer is No. The things of the Spirit do not come naturally, like a mother tongue, to fallen people. Delight and joy and freedom will indeed help me learn, but behind them there does need to be—however much we may wish it were not so—the divine compulsion, the pressure of the Holy Spirit, the restraint of God's firm though loving discipline. Left to ourselves, who knows where "freedom and delight" might take us?

37

What Is God Like?

"Who is Lord beside our Lord? Who is God beside our God?" Yet we long to know what You are like, to understand how it can be that You combine so many apparently conflicting qualities. You are supreme over all, infinitely powerful, utterly merciful, and yet perfectly just. You are able to hide Yourself from us and yet be with us all the time. You are the source of beauty and yet also of raw energy. You are totally reliable and yet we cannot begin to comprehend You. You never change, yet You are the agent of change in everything You have made. Because You are eternal You are neither young nor old, yet You make all things new. And all the while, quietly and unnoticed, You are drawing the proud along the pathway to decay. You are restlessly active and yet the source of rest. You sustain, fill, protect, create, nourish, and perfect all that is.

You love perfectly, but without allowing that love to become an obsession, as we do. You are described as "jealous," but are without hatred or anxiety. You are said to be "angry," but are without sin or distortion. You change Your actions without changing Your purposes.

You have everything, and yet You are pleased to see things flourish. You are in no sense greedy, yet You expect us to give You our talents and our gifts. You owe us nothing, yet You pay off all our debts of failure and sin.

This God is my life, my holy joy. What can I do but praise him?

38

God and the Passing of Time

For all good things come from You, O Lord, and the whole course of my salvation comes from my God.

Your blessings to me began long, long before I could know what they were and where they came from. As a newborn baby, all I knew was how to suck and be content with the result. Later I began to laugh, and, very slowly, by degrees, to discover where I was. But when I wanted to explain my wishes to those around me—parents, nursemaids, and so on—I found I couldn't. I knew what I wanted, but I couldn't communicate with them nor they with me. Consequently, getting very frustrated, I waved my arms, cried, and eventually when none of that succeeded, went into a red-faced rage.

Now that wasn't exceptional, by any means. Ordinary, day-to-day experience tells us that such behavior is common to all babies, but eventually they learn to communicate, and the period of frustration passes.

Yet even as a baby I had a being and a life and desperately wanted to find some way of expressing myself to others. That seems reasonable for a being made in Your image, Lord. You are Yourself

Being and Life, and in Your love You have expressed Yourself to us. You have communicated that being and life to Your creatures.

"Your years do not fail . . . You are still the same." So all Your years are like this present day. We move on from infancy through childhood to each succeeding age, to the point where we are now. But tomorrow, with whatever lies ahead, and yesterday, with all that is past, are contained within this present day of Yours, neither future nor past, but eternally present.

39

Worthy to Be Praised

You are great, O Lord, and worthy to be praised: Your power is great, and Your wisdom endless.

As well as the hosts of heaven, human beings also long to praise You—yes, even we, born to die and burdened with the knowledge of it. We, in our petty pride of life, even we long to praise You. By Your own design, praising You gives us a strange, inexplicable joy, because You have made us for Yourself, and our hearts are restless until they rest in You.

So, Lord, I have two questions. Which should

come first—to turn to You for forgiveness or to praise You for it? And then again, which should be first—to know You or to turn to You?

After all, no one is going to turn to someone they don't know. They will be just as likely to turn to someone or something else. On the other hand, perhaps Your intention is that as we turn to You, as we call to You for help, You will make Yourself known to us. As the apostle Paul wrote, "How shall they call upon him in whom they have not believed? And how shall they believe without a preacher?" But the psalmist stated the other case: "Those who seek the Lord shall praise him . . . Those who seek the Lord shall find him." And, of course, those who find him shall praise him.

So what shall I do? I shall seek You, Lord, by turning to You and calling for Your help. But I shall turn to You in faith, because in fact the truth about You has been preached to me. It is my faith— given by You in the Son of Man, Jesus, and shown to me by the ministry of a faithful preacher—that turns to You and calls to You for help. Faith speaks to faith.

40

Seeing and Believing

Christians believe that, in some sense of the words, we can "see God." We do not think of this, of course, as seeing with our physical eyesight. Nor do we think of it in that other common use of seeing, when we see things in our imagination or understand our actions, intentions, or desires with our mind. "I see" can cover all of those. But it cannot really be used of God, because we do not see him with our eyes, cannot really imagine what he is like, and cannot comprehend him with our minds. So eye, imagination, and intellect are not the means by which we can be said to see God.

Yet Scripture says that the pure in heart shall see God (Matthew 5:8). How can that be? The Scripture cannot lead us astray.

In fact, we often believe things that we have not seen and cannot imagine: that Rome was founded by Romulus, or Constantinople by Constantine; that our parents conceived us, and that we have different and distant ancestors. Now we cannot know these things by sight (we were not around when they happened) nor by our mental reasoning or insight. We have to accept them on the testimony of someone else.

That someone must, of course, be seen by us

as trustworthy, and their testimony must not contradict what we have learned from other sources, already accepted as trustworthy. So things about God that we are shown or told by the testimony of others cannot be accepted if they contradict the Bible.

So what is the connection between seeing and believing? Is the former what we do with something that is present and the latter what we do with something that is absent?

But it is not that simple. After all, I can see with my physical eyes, and hear with my physical ears, someone who is actually present with me as he tries to persuade me to do something. Whether I actually do what he wants or not depends not on his physical presence, nor on my physical awareness of it, but on whether I believe him or not.

And that, in turn, depends on whether the authority by which he urges me to do something seems trustworthy. This is why we believe what the Bible tells us about the creation, or about the resurrection of Jesus, even though we have not seen them with our eyes. We believe the witness to be trustworthy.

So knowledge consists of things seen and things believed. Of the things we see (or have seen in the past) we are our own witnesses. But where the things we believe are concerned, we depend on the witness of others whom we judge to be trustworthy. So it is not unreasonable to argue that belief of that kind is not inferior to seeing, because, in a way, we see with our mental sight—and on appropriate evidence—what we come to believe firmly. Experience may support it, logic may back it up, and it is based on the evidence of those we judge to be totally reliable. We can see things with our eyes and get them quite wrong. We can believe with our minds what we cannot possibly see, and get it right.

As the apostle Peter says, "Though you have never seen him, yet I know that you love him"; and as the Lord himself said, "Blessed are those *who have not seen* but have believed."

41

The Pure in Heart See God

In the Resurrection we shall receive spiritual bodies. This corruptible, mortal body will put on incorruption and immortality: "We shall be changed," as Paul says. And in that new and spiritual body we shall see God.

Now that raises a question at once. We see with our eyes. Does this mean that in heaven we shall have bodies like our earthly ones, complete with physical eyes? Or is there some other way of seeing that does not require a bodily organ to achieve it?

We are told in Scripture that God the Father

sees the Son and that, at the dawn of creation, he saw the light and the skies and the sea and the dry land. Indeed, "God *saw* all the things that he had made and behold they were very good."

But God is spirit. We do not believe him to have a body or to be limited by a physical form. So vision is not attributable only or exclusively to bodies. There must be a way of seeing that is consistent with pure spiritual being. Indeed, all through the Bible that kind of spiritual vision is described, and is regarded as superior to ordinary physical sight. After all, the prophets were called "see-ers."

Having said that, we must be careful not to fall into the opposite error, which is to say that through the resurrection the body not only puts off its mortal and corruptible state, but also the very state of being a body at all, so that in heaven we are *only* spirits. That would be to deny the immortality of the body, which is clearly taught in Scripture. What Paul said was that our bodies at the Resurrection will be *changed*, not cease to exist at all. The Lord Jesus, who is the pattern or prototype of our resurrection, is said to "see the Father" in heaven.

But more important than such questions, to be honest, is this one: What are the conditions to be fulfilled for *us* to see God in heaven? The answer is given us by the Lord himself: "Blessed are *the pure in heart*: They shall see God."

You know how much I admire Bishop Ambrose, because through him the Lord freed me from error and led me to salvation and baptism. I particularly like some words he wrote on this subject—not just because of my personal admiration for him, but because they are based on the truth of Scripture itself.

He wrote, "Even in the resurrection itself it is not easy to see God, except for those who are pure of heart. For the Lord listed many virtuous people who were to be blessed by God, but only the pure in heart would be able to see him."

If, then, only the pure in heart see God, it suggests there are others who will not see him: the unworthy, the impure, and those who do not have a genuine desire to see him.

But the pure in heart *will* see him, and not just at that day of resurrection. They see him when he comes to them and makes his dwelling in their hearts, here and now.

Let us therefore cleanse our hearts and make room for him, so that he may open our eyes and we may see his glory.

42

The Presence of God

Although Almighty God is wholly present everywhere, he does not dwell in everyone. And those in whom he dwells he does not necessarily fill.

It is a truth about God's nature that he fills the entire universe—not by his bulk, as though half of God filled one half and the other half of him the rest of creation, but by the quality of his being. He is the power that sustains it, wholly present in every part of it. As God says through the prophet, "I fill heaven and earth." There is nowhere to go where he is not. "Where can I go from your Spirit, and where can I hide from your presence?"

So isn't it remarkable that the God who fills every part of the universe can be excluded from human hearts that he has made? The apostle Paul speaks of those who "do not have the Spirit of Christ" (Romans 8:9), and, because we believe that the Holy Trinity cannot be divided, it is not possible that God the Father would be present in someone in whom the Holy Spirit does not dwell.

It seems to follow, then, that God is everywhere by the presence of his divine nature, but he is *not* present in every person by the grace of his indwelling. By unbelief and sin we can exclude the Lord of creation from the heart of his creature.

But just as God does not dwell within everyone, so he does not equally fill everyone in whom he does dwell. Otherwise, why should Elisha pray for twice the Spirit of God to be in him that was in Elijah? And how else can we explain that some Christians are clearly holier than others, unless God is dwelling more completely in them?

This raises a further question. If God is wholly present everywhere in his creation, how can it be that he is more or less present in some of his creatures (and not present in some of them at all)?

The answer lies in the capacity of things to receive him, not in his willingness to fill them. The universe, which he made and designated "very good," has the capacity to receive him, so he fills every part of it with his presence and power. But the human spirit, through rebellion and sin, has become wholly *unlike* him, and, apart from forgiveness and grace, lacks the capacity to receive him. If blind eyes cannot receive the light of the sun, it is not the sun's fault. It shines everywhere, but not everything has the capacity to receive its light. So it is with God. If a person, through sin and unbelief, receives less of him, it does not lessen him in any way. God in himself is whole and complete, and does not need to find a dwelling-place in human hearts. Our hearts need *him*, as the means of life and health.

God is eternally reliable, able to be present completely in each individual person. Although each believer may possess him in different degree, according to each one's varied capacities—some more, some less—yet by the grace of his goodness he builds them all up as his most precious temple, the place of his perfect dwelling.

43

In Search of the Land of the Happy Life

If we think of people as travelers at sea, navigating their boats according to different principles of life, we can see at least three types. There are those who set out oblivious of the conditions and end up a little way out to sea, becalmed but in a state of tranquility. They have not expended much effort getting there, but are happy to advise others to join them.

A second group, in contrast, misled by the apparent calm of the sea, strike out for the deeps and get carried far away from their homeland. If some attractive current or wind suddenly carries them along, they happily go with it, even accepting storms and tempests as enjoyable problems. Occasionally, however, a particularly severe setback will drive them at long last to consult their charts, and perhaps even to set course for that safe harbor that they so imprudently left long ago.

The third group consists of those who, having launched out onto the sea in their youth, remember the reliable beacons of their homeland and, fixing their compasses on them, make straight for their home port, despite all distractions of weather or fortune. It is the memory of home that draws them, not the wisdom of experience.

In fact, all of us are really travelers in search of the land of the happy life, the City of God. What we need to know most of all is that blocking the harbor to that land is a mountainous rock rising out of the sea. It should be seriously feared and carefully avoided.

True, it has a very pleasant look about it and is bathed in a deceptively beautiful light. Often those seeking the land of the happy life are foolish enough to think that this mountainous island is preferable to the land itself, thereby losing their ambition to complete the journey. Some are even attracted to leave the land and make for the rock, captivated by its height and by the way it enables them to look down on others. The main danger of this island is that it presents itself as an attractive alternative to seekers who are heading for the happy life but have not yet landed there, and therefore it draws them astray.

All who seek true knowledge of themselves and of God should fear that mountainous island, which is *pride* and *empty glory*. For underneath its ground-crust there is nothing substantial or solid. It collapses under one's feet and swallows up all those who walk on it, consuming them on the threshold of that gleaming and happy land which they had distantly seen but foolishly failed to enter.

44

A Song of Steps:
A Meditation on Psalm 120

This psalm is called a Song of Ascents—a song sung as people climbed upward, step by step, toward the temple. It is a psalm about spiritual progress: progress *upward* from the valley of tears toward the place of blessing. Let us resolve to ascend in heart, since Christ himself descended to earth so that we might ascend to heaven.

We can see among the people of God how true it is that some ascend progressing upward toward God, and some descend, falling back into sin and failure. Those who ascend are those who progress toward spiritual understanding. Those who fall back are those who are satisfied with "milk" when they should be taking spiritual food. It is often fear that holds us back, and it is often wisdom that draws us higher.

So let us imagine ourselves to be the one who is longing to ascend. Where will this ascent take place? In the heart. From where will we begin our ascent? From humility, the valley of tears. And where will we ascend to? To the place described in this psalm as "the place he has appointed."

Now as soon as a Christian sets out seriously to advance in holiness, to "ascend to the place

God has appointed," that person becomes the object of enemy attack, and especially of enemy tongues. Anyone who has never yet experienced such an attack has not yet seriously taken the upward path, and those who are not experiencing it now are not themselves on the way.

But once let Christian men and women set their mind to ascend, to despise worldly and passing values, to put God first and rate pleasure and popularity low, then see how ridicule and criticism are drawn to them. It is not only enemies who attack them. Perhaps more distressing are the negative comments of friends who purport to give them good advice, because to give advice should be an activity of blessing, to help a person toward salvation, whereas these advisers set out to turn their friends away from what is spiritually healthy.

Attacks of this kind, whether from friends or enemies, are called "deceitful tongues" in the Bible. So, before the ascent begins, the psalmist asks for God's help to counter those attacks: "Lord, I called to You in my troubles and You answered me." Why did God answer? To set him on the upward path, to put his feet on the steps that lead higher, to the "place he has appointed." And what was the petition which God answered? "Lord, deliver my soul from unjust lips and from treacherous tongues." It is these tongues that will deter us from the upward climb—these deceitful, flattering, misleading voices. Only God, who calls us higher, can deliver us from them.

45

Sharp Arrows of Love:
A Meditation on Psalm 120:4

What is God's answer to treacherous tongues, to deceitful enemies and unhelpful friends? He himself tells us, "The arrows of the powerful are sharp, like desolating coals." *Desolating* here could equally well be translated "laying waste." The words have similar meaning, because to lay something to waste is to bring desolation.

Let us first consider what these "arrows" are that are God's means of deliverance from treacherous tongues. "The sharp arrows of the powerful" are the words of God. When they are shot, they penetrate right into the heart—but not to bring death, like an ordinary arrow, but to bring love and life. The Lord knows how to fire arrows of love, and no one can shoot a better arrow of love than those who fire the arrow of God's Word. They pierce the heart of the person who loves them, but only to help them love better; and they pierce the heart of the one whose love grows cold in order to fan it back into a blaze.

So words are arrows, but what are these "desolating coals"? They are the burning coals that lay waste our earthly thoughts, clearing away the ground where all those insidious, negative ideas proposed by the treacherous tongues have taken root. You know the sort of thing. God has called us to do something, but we begin to look at and listen to those misleading voices. What makes you think you can do it? And why is it that this other Christian is so much stronger than you? How can this sick man or that impoverished woman achieve so readily what you find so hard? So the Christian is pierced to the heart by God's command, totally discouraged by his or her own hurt pride and human desire to succeed and be well thought of.

It is at this point that the hot coals are applied, burning away the unhealthy vegetation that has overrun the soul—the vegetation of worldly thoughts and ambitions—and clearing the ground so that God can build his temple there. The desolating coals, then, are sent to destroy what has been planted in our hearts by evil.

But coals can be "live." An extinguished coal is called a dead coal, and a glowing one a live coal. So a coal can also be a picture of conversion: of someone who was dead, but is kindled into life by being put alongside a burning coal. The results are sometimes surprising. A drunkard, a villain, a man addicted to the games of the arena, a swindler, can become a committed Christian, fervently serving the Lord, glowing like a live coal.

46

The Tents of Kedar: A Meditation on Psalm 120:5

The psalmist now utters a sad cry. "My soul has wandered far, I have dwelt among the tents of Kedar."

All Christians understand something of this dilemma, for there is a sense in which we live on the earth as "strangers and exiles." We cry out to God "from the ends of the earth." But the exile is not one of fulfillment, but of sorrow. "Alas, my sojourning has become far off."

We find ourselves among "the tents of Kedar." What are they? The word *Kedar* means "darkness," and the tents of Kedar are the tents of Ishmael, the company of those who offer God a carnal, unspiritual, legalistic worship. The psalmist is trapped in a place of spiritual dryness and darkness: "I have dwelt among the tents of Kedar."

His experience there is even more bitter: "With those who hate peace, I was peaceful, and when I spoke to them, they attacked me without cause."

Who hates peace? Surely the person who destroys unity. Unity is peace. Disunity breaks peace. The Lord's will for the church is its peace and unity, and he will in the end judge those who destroy it. But for the present, in the interest of peace, we may be called to "dwell among" them, until that day when God separates the good from the evil and brings only pure grain into the heavenly granaries. So we are peaceful among those who hate peace. These are the words of those who are truly Christ's but are called to live in the midst of chaff.

But still we must bear our witness: Love peace, love Christ—to love peace is to love Christ. Paul tells us that Christ is our peace because he made a unity of two conflicting peoples, "making the two one" (Ephesians 2:14). So we must say to those who claim to be Christ's but hate peace, "Why, if Christ is our peace because he has reunited two peoples into one, do you try to make of one people two? How can you be peacemakers by causing division?" To say this to those who hate peace is to "be peaceful." But when we do say that, these enemies of peace "attack us without cause."

47

The Guard Who Never Sleeps:
A Meditation on Psalm 121

As he ascends step by step in his spiritual pilgrimage to the temple of God, the psalmist prays, "Do not allow my foot to be moved."

Who "moves" our feet? Who moved Adam's feet in Eden, to turn him out of paradise? Surely the same enemy who moves our feet from the safe path. But, first of all, what moved the foot of the angel who fell, with such appalling consequences? We are told in Scripture that he fell *by pride*. Pride turns our steps in the wrong direction, away from God and goodness, away from faith. Faith and trust are the enemies of pride, because faith is an expression of humility: "Under the shadow of Your wings they shall put their trust."

The psalmist expresses his prayer simply: "Do not allow my foot to be moved." God's answer is also simple: "Do not let your guardian fall asleep." If you do not wish to stumble and fall on the upward path, then see that the one who looks after you does not fall asleep. See that he is alert, guarding your every step. Then you will not fall; your foot will not be moved.

But we might well reply, "It's not in our power to insure that our keeper never falls asleep." Of course we don't want our guard to sleep on the task, but how can we prevent it?"

The answer surely is "By choosing the right guardian." Choose a keeper who never sleeps. But is there such a person? Surely everyone has to sleep at some time. The answer is given in the psalm. "Israel's keeper" never sleeps. "He who guards Israel shall neither slumber nor sleep." God does not sleep, he is never off duty, he never rests from his eternal task of guarding and guiding his people.

In his passion the Lord Jesus passed from death to life, opening a way for us who believe in him also to pass from death to life. Many people believe that Christ died: the heathen do, the Jews do, many a wicked person does. Christian faith is distinguished by believing that Christ *rose* from the dead. "Christ, being risen from the dead, dies no more. Death no longer has any power over him."

Death is the ultimate picture of sleep, the final conqueror of mortal beings. If you wish to choose a guard who never sleeps, then choose one who cannot die. Every human being sleeps, and every human being dies. So do not put your confidence in any mortal, but in the Lord Jesus who has conquered death and, like the Father, "never sleeps." "The Lord will guard you"—not a man, who sleeps, slumbers, and dies, but the Lord of life and conqueror of death. He will watch your every step as you climb the hill of the Lord.

48

Going Out and Coming In: A Meditation on Psalm 121:8

"The Lord watch over your coming and going, from this time even for ever more." Let us reflect for a moment on this coming and going. What are they?

I would suggest that for us the *coming* is temptation; and victory over it is the *going*. The Lord, like the potter, places clay vessels into the kiln of testing, and when they are fired, he takes them out. When the potter puts them in, he is not sure of their quality, but he is when he takes them out. The Lord, on the other hand, "knows those who are his," those who will not crack under the heat— and it is the humble ones who best survive the test.

Indeed, in every temptation it is humility that guards us. We climb up from the valley of tears singing the Song of Ascent, and as we do the Lord watches over us to see that we enter his temple safely. "He is faithful," as Paul says, "and will not permit us to be tested beyond our endurance." So the Lord watches over our coming into the place of testing and our going out from it in victory.

Part of that *watching over*, where coming in is concerned, is to remove from us the trial that is beyond our strength. But he also watches over our going out. "He provides a way out, so that you may be able to bear it."

So let us not trust in our own strength to defend ourselves. Rather, let us trust in the Lord to protect and guard us. He does not slumber or sleep— though once he did sleep the sleep of death for us. But now he is risen, never to die again.

As we make our way up from the valley of tears, let us not dawdle or hang back. There is still some way to go, and laziness and pride will try to suggest other and easier ways of getting there. But we can reject them, and climb on steadily toward our goal—if our trust is in the One who watches over our going out and coming in, who guards our feet, and who shields us from the burning sun of day and the chilling moon of night.

If we trust in ourselves, our foot is already "moved," and if it *is* moved, even though we have a degree of faith, pride will cause us to stumble and fall. The one who walks humbly up from the valley of tears toward the hill of the Lord is the one who prays, "Do not let my foot be moved."

49

The Heavenly Jerusalem:
A Meditation on Psalm 122

This, too, is a Song of Ascent. The psalmist wishes to go up, up to heaven or, as it is put here, up to Jerusalem. "I was glad when they said to me, 'Let us go to the house of the Lord'." Like a crowd gathering for a pilgrimage to a holy shrine, the worshipers press forward and upward to the great temple in Jerusalem. They run, they hurry. There is excitement and eagerness. So let us be excited at the prospect of joining God's people and going into his house. Let us rejoice with those who have gone there before us, the prophets and apostles who also call to us, "Let us go to the house of the Lord."

"Our feet were standing in your courts, O Jerusalem." In fact, they have not yet arrived, but such is their faith and hope, it is *as though* their feet are already on the holy ground. You see, you possess the Lord's house if you faithfully seek it. Those who climb upward should encourage themselves by thinking that they are already there. "Our feet stand in your courts." It makes the climb much easier.

But what "Jerusalem" is this? After all, Jerusalem is the name of an earthly city, one that at this time is in ruins. Why should we long to stand in a ruined and desolate foreign city? But the psalmist, through the Spirit, does not sing of the earthly Jerusalem, built of stones and wood and mortar—the Jerusalem that "kills the prophets and stones those sent to her"—but of the heavenly Jerusalem, the one that Paul called "the mother of us all . . . eternal in the heavens."

This Jerusalem is described here as "being built as a city." When David spoke those words, the city of Jerusalem was already built. The city that was still being built was the new Jerusalem, the one built not with bricks but with living stones (as Peter says), built the foundation of Jesus Christ. It is a city in the heavens, with a heavenly foundation. Every preacher of the truth helps to cut the stones, but it is the Lord himself who shapes them into his building. If we have faith, then we are part of the building toward which we press. "You are built as living stones . . . You are the temple of God."

That city is marked by one shining quality: "Jerusalem is built as a city that is at unity with itself." All its inhabitants are in unity. Like the Lord who made it, it is always the same, not now one thing and then something else. God is One, and always the same. Christ is One, and always the same. And if we, under the pressure of daily life with all its passing values and changing circumstances, feel that we are variable, inconsistent, then let us remember that if we cannot ascend, *he* descended. He came to us—the one who is "eternally the same"—to make us what we cannot make ourselves.